Battleground Europe

ASIAGO

15/16 June 1918
Battle in the Woods and Clouds

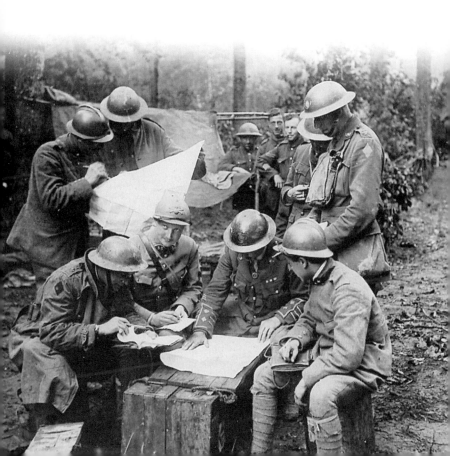

With the continued expansion of the Battleground series a
Battleground Series Club has been formed to benefit the reader. The
purpose of the Club is to keep members informed of new titles and to
offer many other reader-benefits. Membership is free and by
registering an interest you can help us predict print runs and thus assist
us in maintaining the quality and prices at their present levels.

Please call the office 01226 734555, or send your name and address
along with a request for more information to:
Battleground Series Club Pen & Sword Books Ltd,
47 Church Street, Barnsley, South Yorkshire S70 2AS

Battleground Europe

ASIAGO

15/16 June 1918
Battle in the Woods and Clouds

Francis Mackay

LEO COOPER

To the 'Flo'ers o' the Forest'; the dead of all nations buried among the woods and clouds on the Asiago plateau.

15/16 June 1918 Battle in the Woods and Clouds
The Battle of Asiago was a battalion commanders' and soldiers' battle, and not only a battle in the clouds and mist like Chattanooga, but also a battle in the woods.
OH Mil Ops, Italy 1915-1919 Brig-Gen S Edmonds; p. 201

Chattanooga, Tennessee, September 1863: Confederate troops lead by General Braxton Bragg defeated Federal forces under General William S Rosecrans.

First published in 2001 by
LEO COOPER
an imprint of
Pen & Sword Books Limited
47 Church Street, Barnsley, South Yorkshire S70 2AS

ISBN 0 85052 759 7

A CIP catalogue record of this book is available
from the British Library

Printed by CPI UK.

*For up-to-date information on other titles produced under the Leo Cooper imprint,
please telephone or write to:*

Pen & Sword Books Ltd, FREEPOST, 47 Church Street
Barnsley, South Yorkshire S70 2AS
Telephone 01226 734222

CONTENTS

Introduction by Series Editor

It has long been an intention to move the detailed surveys of Great War battles in the *Battleground Europe* Series out of the Western Front and to other theatres of the war. Italy has won the race, but we hope that it will not be long before more detailed volumes on the Gallipoli campaign make their appearance.

Asiago was not a particularly big battle from the British perspective, essentially using troops - to all intents and purposes - from two Divisions: the 23rd and the 48th (South Midlands). But the battlefield lent itself readily to this type of book, being reasonably compact and significantly undeveloped since the events of June 1918. The contrast between the rolling countryside of the Somme and around Cambrai and the flatlands of Flanders and that of this northern Italian mountainous region could not be much greater. Different countryside and a different foe meant different fighting methods, and by and large the British adapted well to the new requirements.

Although not particularly well known today, the fighting at Asiago was recorded for posterity by Hugh Dalton and Norman Gladden; whilst Vera Brittan's brother was killed in the fighting of June 1918. One of the values of this book is being able to put yourself as accurately as practicable on the spots where these men were during the confusion of battle and the relative tranquillity of the daily trench routine.

An interesting point is that this book came about largely because the author was on duty with British forces engaged in missions in Bosnia and Kosovo; a new military generation introduced to what had become a fading sideshow to the controversies raging over the Western Front. It is to be hoped that this book will help to ensure that the forces in Italy during the Great War are not forgotten.

Nigel Cave
Casta Natale, Rovereto.

Acknowledgements

This guide could not have been written without the assistance of many people in Britain and Italy. Regimental secretaries and curators of regimental museums have patiently steered me through their archives. Colonel John Lowes and Lieutenant-Colonel Pat Love, of the Worcestershire Regimental HQ, were of particular help and I am indebted to them, and the Regiment, for permission to reproduce photographs, maps and quotations. Cliff Housley, Regimental Historian of The Sherwood Foresters, was a mine of information about the 11th Battalion at San Sisto Ridge, and the life and times of Lieutenant-Colonel CE Hudson, VC DSO and Bar, MC; my thanks go to the Regiment for permission to quote from the battalion history, *The Men from the Greenwood,* and to reproduce photographs of Lieutenant Colonel Hudson and Captain Edward Brittain. Captain PHD Marr, of the Fusiliers Museum of Northumberland, provided much useful information, sometimes at short notice. In the matter of divisional and unit histories, and personal accounts of service in Italy, my thanks go to Gill Blackwell, Librarian, Military Affairs Reference Service, HQ Land Command, Wilton, and her colleagues in the Prince Consort's Library, Aldershot; also to Rosemary Rennie, of Cambusbarron Library. The staff of the Imperial War Museum were also helpful to me, especially those in the Department of Printed Books and the Photographic Archive. Dave Buxton devilled in the PRO, frequently at short notice, and John Wilks kindly explained some aspects of the Battle of Caporetto. The phrase *'Last Battles of The Risorgimento'* is unashamedly borrowed from *The British Army in Italy 1917-1918* by John and Eileen Wilks. Dr Alf Peacock gently guided my use of English; during the Great War his father served in the 8th (S) Bn King's Own Yorkshire Light Infantry in Italy, and spent many weary days on the Asiago plateau.

The Commonwealth War Graves Commission staff at Maidenhead, and cemetery custodians in the Veneto, were always co-operative and are a credit to the organization. The work of the custodians is always visible to visitors but seldom acknowledged in print, so the opportunity has been taken to include a photograph of one of the Italian team whose efforts in the Asiago area make the cemeteries a pleasure to visit.

I wish to acknowledge, with thanks, permission from the following bodies or individuals to quote from the under-noted works: HMSO for permission to quote from Norman Gladden, *Across the Piave,*

Worcestershire Regiment (various sources). Hodder Headline Publishing Group for permission to use the map *German relief, Caporetto, 1917,* originally published in Holger H Herwig *The First World War, Germany and Austria-Hungary*; *Azienda Promozione Turistica di Altopiano di Asiago* for permission to use the schematic map of the Asiago plateau; Gino Rossato, of *Edizioni Gino Rossato,* Chris Coogan, Vittorio Cora, Pete Helmore, David Thistlethwaite for permission to use some of their photographs, and David Helmore for photographing the Asiago medal. I have been unable to trace the copyright holder for *With British Guns to Italy,* by Hugh Dalton, but am grateful to the Random House Group for their advice. Richard Jeffs, of the Oxfordshire and Buckinghamshire Light Infantry Regimental Museum, and Lawrie Pettit, an authority on awards and medals for members of the British Forces in Italy during the Great War, were of particular help, as were Jim Ure and Dale Hjort, true experts on the campaign. The trustees of the *Museo Storico Della Guerra,* Canove, especially Francesco Magnaboschi, provided unflagging support.

My thanks for their forbearance go to many NATO colleagues in Vicenza who saw more old battlefields than perhaps they might have wished, and learned the hard way that our grandfathers were a tough lot as they walked up the escarpment in five hours. Luitenant-Kolonel Hans Boetier, Royal Netherlands Army, introduced me to Asiago, and explained some aspects of artillery fire control in forests and mountains.

In the Veneto, Vittorio Cora of Asiago, an expert on the Great War, especially the battles on his beloved plateau, was an inspiring guide. Tiziano Palumbo of Montebelluna patiently explained the logistics of

CWGC Custodian, Asiago Sr. Claudio Magnaboschi.

the retreat from Caporetto and the battle of the Piave. Claudio Cappozo of Lugo di Vicenza rescued my wife and I after a mountain boulder hit our car, and later showed me the remnants of British supply sites in Calvene and Lugo di Vicenza. All three bore with fortitude my attempts to speak their beautiful language.

The staff at Pen and Sword have been enormously patient; I am grateful for their courage in proceeding with another book about an overlooked campaign. The information belongs to the fore-mentioned, any sins of commission or omission are mine, so any amendments or comments will be welcome.

8

Foreword
by
Brigadier JCL King MBE
Commander 143 (West Midlands) Brigade

On first acquaintance the picturesque scenery of the Asiago Plateau must have come as a respite to the men of the 143rd (Warwickshire) Infantry Brigade and their compatriots in the 7th, 23rd and 48th (South Midlands) Divisions. All were more familiar with the mud and slaughter of the Western Front than the rolling green pastures and wooded slopes of the *Altopiano.*

Yet as the winter of 1917/18 began to bite, the men would face conditions and fighting as hazardous as the Western Front and over six hundred would find their last resting place in the area of 'woods and clouds'.

As Francis Mackay makes clear in this readable, fascinating and often poignant battlefield guide, the Italians have not forgotten the sacrifice of eighty two years ago. I have visited the Asiago battlefield twice in my capacity as Commander of the present-day 143rd Brigade and was struck by the friendliness of the people of the *Setti Commune* and by their knowledge of, and

Brigadier General JCL. King MBE.

interest in, the events of 15/16 June 1918 - the 'Battle in the Woods and Clouds'. We, too, will not forget the sacrifice of our forebears during their gallant defence of a critical point in the Allied line.

John King,
Shrewsbury,
March 2000.

Introduction

This is the first guide of the **Battleground Europe** series to examine the First World War Italian Front. This long-neglected campaign saw ferocious fighting between the Italian and the Austro-Hungarian armies in some of the most rugged terrain in Europe, where the weather and the mountains were as much a danger as the enemy. Other volumes are planned to cover engagements involving British, French and American forces as well as purely Italian-Austrian ones.

A small British expeditionary force fought in Italy alongside the Italians amid scenes of outstanding beauty, especially the site of the Battle of Asiago, 15/16 June 1918. This book gives an outline of the British part in the battle, and provides a simple guide to key areas. It does not describe in detail why Italy joined the Allies in 1915, or the struggles between the Italian and Austro-Hungarian Armies before British and French troops arrived in late 1917. It deals with a short engagement in a larger battle (the Battle of the Piave), one which, had the results been different, could have lost the Allies the war. The battle (and the campaign) are almost unknown to British military historians, enthusiasts, and servicemen. This is a pity, as it was not only an interesting engagement but the battlefield is easily accessible and remarkably intact, especially the section defended by the British in 1918. Readers unfamiliar with the campaign are recommended to read the *Official History Military Operations Italy 1915-1919,* available from the Imperial War Museum or Naval & Military Press, and *The British Army in Italy, 1915-1918,* by John and Eileen Wilks and published by Pen & Sword.

British ground forces fought in three small areas of northern Italy. Firstly, some Royal Garrison Artillery batteries supported Italian forces near Trieste; secondly, infantry divisions operated in the mountains north-west of Venice; and then thirdly, along the River Piave. In mid-1918, one hundred and twenty thousand British troops were serving in Italy and over 2,000 died there. The intervention of British (and French) forces was crucial to Italy's war effort, and the Italians have not forgotten, as hundreds of names in the visitors books at CWGC cemeteries testify.

The Italians, British and French were eventually joined by the US 332nd Infantry Regiment, the Czech 'Storm Corps' and detachments of Rumanians and Southern Slavs (Croats, Slovenes, Bosnians), deserters from the Austro-Hungarian Armies. Italian troops served in Salonika, Gallipoli and France (where over 4,000 died), and a desert-trained unit from Italy's colony in Libya served in Egypt and Palestine.

Five VCs were awarded during the campaign, including two for bravery in the Battle of Asiago. A Battle Honour, Piave, was awarded

to twenty-two regiments for action in the battle.

The *Official History* concedes (pg 201) that the fighting in the battle was generally so confused that it is almost impossible to trace exactly movements of the units involved. This is especially true of the fighting in the forested area defended by the 48th Division. If more attention has been lavished on one brigade, and on one battalion, than on others, it is due to lack of space to describe accurately a complex and confused engagement. The whole Battle of the Piave deserves closer examination, and this guide only provides an outline of the British role in the 'battle in the woods and clouds'.

Please note that 'Austro-Hungary' appears as 'Austria'; that the Empire's three armies - the Common Army *(Kaiserlich und Königlich Heer)*, the Austrian *Landwehr* and the Hungarian *Honved*, appear collectively as *'k.u.k.'*, and 'Barental' is used, *(Barenthal* on some maps) likewise 'Pria dell'Acqua', not Pria dell'acqua. Monte (eg Monte Kaberlaba) appears as M. and Casa (House) as C. Map grids are at 1,000 metres.

Advice for Tourists

Location: The Asiago plateau lies at the western end of the escarpment backing the Venetian plain. It is 121 kilometres from Venice, 106 from Verona, 190 from the Brenner Pass, 240 from Milan and 55 from Vicenza.

Access. The plateau is, unfortunately, not suitable for disabled travellers.

Maps: Walking maps of the plateau can be obtained from The Map Shop, 15 High Street, Upton on Severn, WR8 0HJ. The **Kompass** 1:50,000 *No 78 - Altopiano dei Sette Comuni* shows CWGC Cemeteries. The Asiago tourist board provides an excellent **Great War 1915-1918 Map.** In Italy, look for **VICENZA** Carta della Provincia, which also shows CWGC cemeteries on the plateau.

Travel Air: BA and Alitalia fly to Verona and Venice; Go and Ryanair also serve Venice. Various charter companies service both cities.

Car: First-time tourers should note that driving in Italy is brisker than in the UK (or the US and Canada)! Read all information available before departing, especially about buying fuel. Most non-autostrada petrol stations close for lunch and on Mondays, and not all accept credit-cards. If touring in summer, take/buy car sun-shades. In Asiago, a 'Saturday market' is held in the main car-park on the *Viale Giacomo Matteoti.* Park elsewhere on a Friday night otherwise your car will be removed.

Non-drivers. The tours described here are mainly for car-users, but the routes can be followed by cyclists, and walkers. Access to the plateau for non-drivers can be gained by train to Thiene via Vicenza, then bus to Asiago, or to Bassano del Grappa via Padua, then bus; or train from Verona to Trento and bus to Asiago

Weather: The plateau is 3,300 feet above sea level so is very cold in winter, with heavy snowfalls, but warm in summer. The best time to go is late spring or September, when the air is like champagne (well, *Prosecco*) after the lowland smog. Damp winds coming off the Adriatic provide plenty of moisture, either thick mist or torrential rain. Beware of sudden thunder or hail storms as they are fierce and frightening; in late June 1999 hailstones measuring 2.5cms fell one afternoon on the southern hills.

Exploring: The plateau is busy most week-ends, and throughout the summer, but very quiet in late spring and autumn, when only the woods are busy with mushroom pickers. Fires are restricted to concrete road-side barbecue stands and fireplaces in *rifugio*, shelters for storm-bound walkers, cyclists and drivers. The forest tracks can be closed to vehicles at short notice due to timber harvesting; keep well clear of the sound of chain-saws! Mountain bikes, ideal for exploring the battlefield, can be hired in Asiago.

Language: Few people in the Veneto speak English. A smile, mime and a dictionary get you through most situations. [*'Scusi, Inglesi, non parliamo italiano'*, is more tactful than "Do you speak English?"]

Tourist board: The *Azienda di Promozione Turistica Altipiano di Asiago* has two offices in Asiago, one in the lovingly restored railway station, the other in the Town Hall, on the main square, the Piazza Carli. They are manned by charming girls who speak English and are very helpful to those interested in the *Grande Guerra*. The *Azienda* will supply brochures, maps and accommodation lists by mail, but cannot book accommodation, only forward requests to hotels, camp-sites or holiday apartments. E-mails and faxes are dealt with promptly by the AZT, but Italian postal services can be very slow.

Comune di Asiago - Ufficio del Turismo
Piazza Carli - 36012 - ASIAGO (VI) Italia
http://www.comune.asiago.vi.it
e-mail: asiagoturismo@comune.asiago.vi.it
Tel: 0049 0424 462221   fax: 0049 0424 462445.

Accommodation:

The area has many excellent hotels, and most proprietors or managers speak a little English, and there is usually a member of staff, or someone living nearby, who can help in case of difficulty. In Asiago, the owner of the Hotel Alpi, Sr Marco Ambrosini, speaks English. He is chairman of the local branch of the Italian Infantry Association, and organizes the annual Magnaboschi commemoration service mentioned later.

http://www.
e-mail: hotelapiasiago@tiscalinet.it

Battlefield tours:

Tour companies, such as Flanders Tours, (01480 890966), and the War Research Society (0121 430 5348) are beginning to take an interest in the area. Look in 'Battlefields Review' (Wharncliffe Publishing Ltd, 01226 734222), Western Front Association bulletins:

Membership Secretary: [2000] Stuart Bufton, Harkaway Cottage, Winston, Stowmarket, IP14 6LQ.

Health and Safety:

There are no special health hazards in northern Italy, but tourers should take a Form E111, and have current anti-tetanus jabs. There is a good hospital in Asiago, but at the time of writing not many of the staff speak English. However, the main hospital in Vicenza has an English-speaking doctor available day and night, because of the nearby NATO bases. Observe the usual safety rules when walking in forests or along mule-tracks on the escarpment. Strong footwear and a walking pole/stick are essential, also head-cover, sun-glasses, sun block and plenty to drink. Keep out of dug-outs. Do not pick up anything remotely like a shell, grenade or bomb, and watch out for barbed wire: much of the original is still hidden in undergrowth. The trenches are deep, damp and slippery.

Food and drink:

The local produce is excellent. A corkscrew is vital, a cool-bag and kitchen knife useful. The cheese factory-cum-supermarket west of Asiago is a trencherman's delight, but the staff seemingly do not speak English. There is a good delicatessen in Asiago, on the Corso IV Novembre, which has a *rotisserie* service at week-ends and other busy times. Most cafes and shops close on Mondays!

Chapter One

SETTING THE SCENE
Italy, Austria and the Asiago Plateau

August 1914 found Italy an interested, if apprehensive, spectator of the unfolding world tragedy. She was friendly with France and Britain, but bound to Germany and Austria by the Triple Alliance. That, however, only required signatories to assist each other if attacked, and as Austria and Germany were aggressors, Italy opted for neutrality. The belligerents cast around for allies, and Switzerland and Italy, each bordering France and one or both of the Central Powers, were wooed by both sides. The Swiss remained steadfastly neutral but Italy wavered as she longed to regain *Italia Irredenta,* to redeem Italian-speaking provinces ruled by Austria. The Germans did not mind parting with Austrian territory, but their ally, beset with nationalist movements, objected: relinquishing even one hectare could have lead to the empire disintegrating. The Allies, able to offer enemy territory, could afford to be generous, and won the bidding. In May 1915 Italy declared war on Austria (but not on Germany, that came later), and joined the Allies, who promptly established Military Missions in Rome, and sent Liaison Officers to field (Army, Corps) headquarters.

The Austrians, preoccupied with disastrous campaigns in the east, had neither the intention nor the forces to attack Italy. Later, certainly, when Russia and Serbia were crushed. The Italians, however, wanted

A topographical map illustrating the 1915 frontier between Italy and Austria.

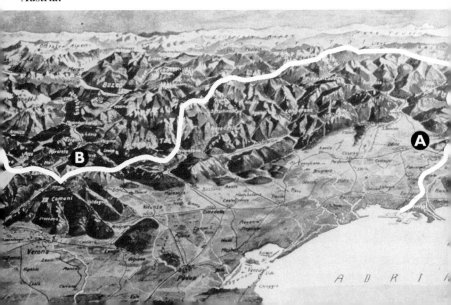

Typical Altipiano scenery, Folgaria Plateau. DALE HJORT.

to attack and had forces at hand, but the options open to them were limited. The frontier with Austria, 375 miles long, meandered from Switzerland to the Adriatic through some of the most rugged terrain in Europe. But the mountains that hemmed the Italians in also kept the Austrians out. The few natural invasion routes, such as the Adige valley, were death traps, covered by the guns of modern forts. Everywhere else invaders faced sheer slopes, surmountable only by lightly-armed mountain troops. So each side had the same problem: how to penetrate the mountain ring with sufficient force to win a major battle, without being outflanked.

At only two places along the entire frontier was there ground remotely suitable for an offensive by either side. The first lay at the eastern end of the frontier, **(A)** on photo, page 15, where it left the mountains to reach the Adriatic. Here there was room for manoeuvre, and for the proper deployment of armies for an offensive into the enemy heartland. But to the east loomed the Julian Alps, presenting the same problems as the rest of the frontier photo, whichever way an invader was heading .

The second place lay north-west of Venice, where a freak of nature has created foot-steps over the mountains **(B)** on photo, page 15. Four rocky shelves, the *Altipiano* (plateaux) of Folgaria, Lavarone, Luserna and Asiago, link the Val d'Adige, and the Val Sugana, vital Austrian supply routes, to the Venetian Plain. The plateaux provide a relatively easy invasion route - *compared with anywhere else along the frontier.* And once over the northern mountains of the plateaux only a few hilly kilometres kept an invader from the enemy's backyard. For the Austrians that meant the Italian supply routes; and for the Italians the rear of the Austrian frontier defences, and their supply line from Innsbruck, Germany and the rest of Austro-Hungary. It also offered a

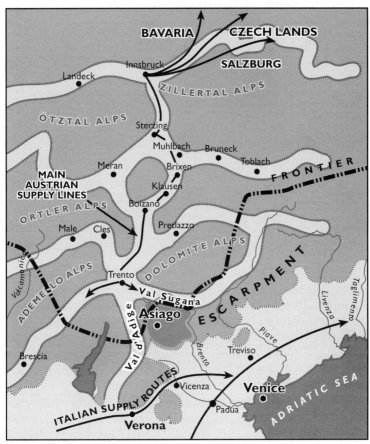

Strategic location of the plateaux showing pre 1915 Austro-Italian Frontier.

possible invasion route into western Austria and Bavaria. (The Germans were aware of that threat, remote though it appeared in 1915. Early in November 1918 they moved troops to Bavaria when the Austrians were clearly about to capitulate. The Italians had a plan ready for such an attack, for which they wanted some British troops.) In 1915 the frontier between Italy and Austria cut across the plateaux, placing the Austrians within tantalizing sight of the plains. But while they controlled the three lower northern levels, the Italians held the fourth and most important, the Asiago plateau.

The Asiago plateau

The full name is *Altopiano di Setti Commune,* 'Plateau of the Seven Municipalities'; Asiago, Conco, Enego, Foza, Gallio, Lusiana, Roana and Rotzo [eight - but that's how the tourist board describes it!] In the north, from the Val Sugana, mountains rise to 6500 feet. The central

Panorama of the *Altopiano*, looking north from Vicenza. AZT.

plain, 3,300 feet above sea level, is rolling pasture land, bisected by the river Ghelpac and gouged at each end by defiles, the Val d'Assa and the Val Franzela. To the south are low hills, then the escarpment, a seeming-vertical wall of rock and forest, threaded with mule tracks (*mulaterria*). The track of a defunct narrow-gauge rack and pinion railway climbs the escarpment; it ran from Rochette to Asiago, and during the Great War was a key Allied supply route.

The *Altopiano* has a long and interesting history. There are Neolithic cave paintings in the Ghelpac Gorge, and the remains of Iron Age settlements near Roanna. Dante was so awe-struck by the gloomy Val d'Assa that it appears in *The Divine Comedy* as the 'Mouth of Hell'. Between 1310 and 1807 the *Altopiano* was an independent state, the 'Honourable Regency of the Seven Municipalities', one of the earliest confederations in Europe. During Napoleon's Italian adventure it vanished, along with its main trading partner, the Most Serene Republic of Venice. But dreams of independence lingered and in 1945 some wanted to turn the *Altopiano* into another San Marino, the tiny idependent republic embedded in Italy some 300km to the south.

Profile of the Asiago Plateau.

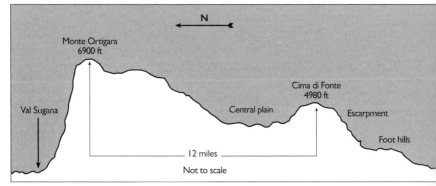

The Asiago escarpment, looking north from Vicenza. FRANCIS MACKAY.

The Asiago plateau is a place apart, a wooded haven in the clouds, but between 1915 and 1918 it was a battlefield, and became the last resting-place for Austrians, Bosnians, Czechs, Dalmatian Croats, Frenchmen, Hungarians, Italians, Rumanians, Slovenes, Galician Poles, a few Americans, and for more than six hundred British servicemen, many killed or missing in the Battle of Asiago. This is, in part, their story.

British troops make friends with Italian gunners on their way from the front line. TAYLOR LIBRARY.

Chapter Two

ITALY v AUSTRIA 1915-1917
The Last Battles of the *Risorgimento*

The Italians

In 1915 the Italian army was recovering from winning a war with
Turkey over the control of Libya, and was short of men and material.
Fortunately in July 1914 a new and reforming Chief of Staff had been
appointed who was able to use the war-scare of that year to wring funds
from parliament. General Count Luigi Cadorna was an able and
energetic administrator who achieved much before Italy entered the
war. New weapons were purchased, supply procedures improved and
soldiers recruited. As a sensible precaution during the period of
neutrality the frontier defences were strengthened, especially on the
Asiago plateau.

The plateau defences

The Italian Corps of Engineers, regarded by contemporaries as
among the best in the world, also improved access to the plateau.
Mulaterria were improved and exposed roads camouflaged. Cart-
tracks winding up the escarpment became roads, and on the plateau a
cow-path was transformed into the Barental Road, later familiar to
thousands of British soldiers. On the Venetian plain narrow-gauge
railways cut across fields and through vineyards to supply depots and
dumps in foothill villages. From there the engineers erected cable-
ways to hoist supplies up to the plateau. *Teleferiche* (*Seilbahnen* to the

**War-road to Asiago under construction across the escarpment, above
Marostica, 1915.** MUSEO STORICO DELLA GUERRA, CANOVE

Mulaterria **under construction.** GINO ROSSATO

Austrians) were under-rated by the British, but the Italians and Austrians had their operation down to a fine art. Later in the war a sort of trolley-bus system, a *filovia,* hauled supplies up to the plateau and troops down to the plains.

The plateau is composed of limestone so has little surface water apart from some open pools, similar to dew-ponds, and the Ghelpac, which has little running water for most of the year. The *genio* built a water distribution system, the *Impianti Idrici,* to pump water from the river Astico 2,500ft up to, and across, the plateau to reservoirs and distribution points.

The Austrians

After ten months of war the armed forces of His Majesty the Emperor of Austria and Apostolic King of Hungary, Franz Josef I, were in poor shape and badly led. The Emperor was nominally head of the *k.u.k,* with a deputy, Archduke Ferdinand, in the position of *Armeeoberkommandant* (Commander in Chief of the Armies in the

Camouflaged mountain road. FRANCIS MACKAY.

Teleferiche, near M. Corno (Tattenham Corner, British sector). VITTORIO CORA

Field). The real power lay with the *Chef des General Stabes für die gesamte bewaffnete Macht* (Chief of the General Staff), *Generaloberst* Franz Baron Conrad von Hotzendorf, a highly intelligent, thrusting officer. He was a jingoist, and a vocal advocate of war as a solution to the Empire's political problems, and disliked the Italians. He was an innovator, having pre-1914 created the crack Austrian mountain warfare units, as he had long recognized that war with Italy was inevitable. In fact he welcomed it as he wanted to emulate the great *Feldmarschal* Radetzky, many time trouncer of Italian armies.

Italian army water-point, Granezza, Asiago plateau. VITTORIO CORA.

Unfortunately Conrad had the Austrian generals' *'ineradicable habit of being defeated'* (Marshal Suvaroff). Several post-war military observers considered him the best strategist of the war, but he was, to put it mildly, unlucky, and failed to understand his armies' limitations, the inadequacies of the imperial administration, and weakness of the empire's munitions industries.

Feldmarschal Franz Baron Conrad von Hotzendorf.

The Austro-Hungarian Army.

In *k.u.k* was an amazing mixture of humanity. The soldiers were drawn from nineteen nationalities, mobilization notices had been printed in fifteen languages and field postcards in three. There were three official languages: German, Hungarian and Serbo-Croat, and about sixteen 'regimental languages'. One Slovakian battalion reportedly used English as many of the soldiers were learning it before emigrating to America!

In 1915 the *k.u.k,* weakened by huge losses in Russia and Serbia, was faced with a new front. The defences along the frontier with Italy had been lightly manned by territorial units and reservists, but as war approached the *k.u.k* somehow found the men to reinforce the garrisons and create a small reserve.

Opening moves

Cadorna planned several attacks along the frontier, with the main offensive in the east, across the Isonzo River. The Italian army repeatedly attacked on this front, the twelve Battles of the Isonzo, which gained some ground at the expense of enormous casualties. Other parts of the frontier also saw action, with some gains for the Italians, and some losses, including the northern half of the Asiago plateau. Here, in May 1916, the Austrian launched the *Strafexpediton* (Punishment Expedition), intended to cut off all Italian forces east of Venice. The Austrian offensive failed to reach the Venetian plains, but pushed the Italians out of the northern mountains and into the southern hills.

Asiago front

The *k.u.k.* established a front line across the middle of the plateau, running from the Val Brenta, via Asiago, the Ghelpac Gorge and the

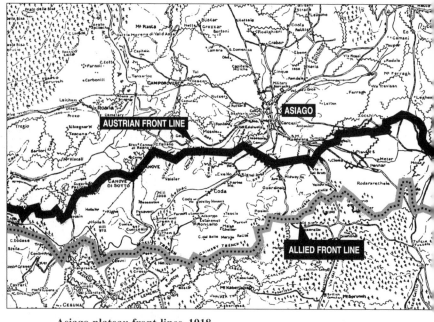

Asiago plateau front-lines, 1918.

K.u.k engineers: 'Gesteinsbohrzuge' (rock-drilling team). GINO ROSSATO.

lower Val d'Assa to the Val d'Astico. This new line was a nightmare for supply officers as everything had to travel across the central plain. The last stages of this journey were mainly in full view of the Italians so supplies and reinforcements could only be moved at night or in mist, or by paths cut into the sides of the Val d'Assa.

The Italians established a front line along the southern edge of the plain and both armies burrowed into the rock. Engineers drilled, blasted and gouged trenches, dugouts (*Fuchslöcher* – fox-holes) and *Seilbahn* stations. The Austrians built new roads and *Seilbahnen,* and incorporated captured sections of the *Impianti Idrici* into their own water distribution system.

Caporetto

In the Eleventh Battle of the Isonzo (August-September 1917) the Italians advanced a remarkable ten kilometres until halted by an effort which almost broke the Austrians. They sought, and received, German help, but lost control of the operation. A German mountain warfare expert, Lieutenant-General Krafft von Delmensingen, assessed the situation and identified the area on either side of the small town of Caporetto as the best point for an attack. It was lightly held, and although hardly ideal for an offensive, offered some chance of success. The attack on Caporetto was part of a wider offensive along the Isonzo front by thirty *k.u.k* and seven German divisions, six especially released by Ludendorff from his meagre strategic reserve. Two of these German divisions came from Riga, where they had been involved in a devastating attack on the Russian defences. The offensive was

German relief; Caporetto 1917.

preceded by an elaborate deception plan, but the Italians soon learned of the proposed assault. Cadorna correctly identified the area around Caporetto as his Achilles heel and ordered the defences to be strengthened. Unfortunately these orders were not obeyed, and the rest is history.

On 24 October 1917, a well-planned, meticulously organized and vigorously prosecuted (which included a certain *Oberleutnant* Erwin Rommel) attack fell on the unfortunate Italian Second Army. By 10 November 1917, the Italians had withdrawn across the Piave. When the Austrian and German forces reached the Piave they were exhausted and starving. They tried to cross the river but were repelled and lapsed into the boredom of static defence. The opposing armies dug in, re-grouped, trained and took what shelter they could from the elements and enemy gunfire. Cadorna was replaced by General Armando Diaz. The leaders sat down and wondered what to do next; the soldiers sat and shivered. The scene was set for the next act, the next throw of the dice.

Restored Austrian trenches, M. Zebio, north of Asiago. FRANCIS MACKAY

Austrian dug-out M. Zebio. It was hewn out of solid rock and could hold one infantry company (200 men). FRANCIS MACKAY

Chapter Three

ALLIED ASSISTANCE
Autumn 1917-Spring 1918

Call for help

General Cadorna had his failings but knew when to ask for help, and had the courage to do so from allies. By last light on 24 October he realized the attack on Caporetto posed a threat to the entire front, and advised the Allied Military Missions accordingly. Fortunately their governments had plans ready, and reacted quickly. By the time the Italian rearguard crossed the Piave three French divisions were already in Italy and three more were arriving. The British 23rd and 41st Divisions were in transit, the 7th and 48th packing and the 2nd, 5th, 21st and 47th under orders to move, although only the 5th eventually went to Italy.

The five British divisions were organized into a compact force of two Corps (XI and XIV) supported by a full range of arms and services, including an RFC brigade. The Italian Expeditionary Force was controlled by GHQ, British Forces Italy, which also administered a railway supply route for Salonika and Egypt which ran from France to Taranto, and rest camps for those theatres at Faenza, in cenral Italy. By mid-November the British had congregated near Padua, where they were joined by some RGA heavy batteries sent to the Isonzo front in April 1917 in response to an earlier appeal from the Italians, and which had been caught up in the retreat following Caporetto.

The effect on the Italians of the sight of thousands of smart, healthy

Pipes and drums of 2/KOSB, Italy, winter 1917. TAYLOR COLLECTION.

and cheerful British troops marching towards the sound of the enemy guns was electric. The populace suddenly realized their nation was not struggling alone, and that help was to hand. The British troops were given a rapturous, if sometimes bemused, welcome by Italians who had rarely met so many foreigners, and at such close quarters. Some of these foreign soldiers wore skirts! And short ones, too! *Elora!* For their part the British were amazed at some Italian habits. The *Official History* recorded that

General Plumer.
TAYLOR LIBRARY.

> *Another difficulty experienced in co-operating with the Italians was their habit of closing down all business from 12 to 3 pm every day for the midday meal and rest, a habit continued even when the war was not going too well for them; as the Austrians knocked off at 11.30 am for a couple of hours the cause did not suffer. As noon approached Italian officers very obviously became uneasy and wanted to stop any work at hand. All that was to change in the near future.*

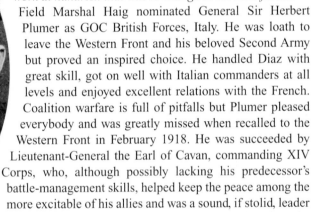

Field Marshal Haig nominated General Sir Herbert Plumer as GOC British Forces, Italy. He was loath to leave the Western Front and his beloved Second Army but proved an inspired choice. He handled Diaz with great skill, got on well with Italian commanders at all levels and enjoyed excellent relations with the French. Coalition warfare is full of pitfalls but Plumer pleased everybody and was greatly missed when recalled to the Western Front in February 1918. He was succeeded by Lieutenant-General the Earl of Cavan, commanding XIV Corps, who, although possibly lacking his predecessor's battle-management skills, helped keep the peace among the more excitable of his allies and was a sound, if stolid, leader

Lord Cavan.

of the British force. Among his staff was Edward, Prince of Wales, who did not enjoy his time in Italy.

XI Corps (5th and 41st Divisions) returned to France in Spring 1918, leaving XIV Corps (7th, 23rd and 48th Divisions), usually referred to by the Italians as the *Corpo Britannico* as there was an Italian XIV Corps nearby.

Into the mountains

In late March 1918, after a spell in trenches along the Piave, the

British and the French corps deployed onto the Asiago plateau as part of the Italian Sixth Army (Lieutenant-General Luca Montuori), in preparation for an offensive later cancelled. This was intended to push the *k.u.k.* off the plateau, then destroy the huge supply centres around Trento and threaten the entire enemy mountain front.

The British sector

The British were on the left of the Sixth Army front, with the French on their right. On the British left was the Italian First Army, defending the western end of the plateau and the Val d'Astico. The British sector was about three miles wide, but the front line was nearly five miles long due to the undulating nature of the ground. The right boundary ran alongside Barental Road past the Granezza HQ complex to the escarpment. [See map page 31] The left boundary started at the Ghelpac Gorge near its junction with the Ronco valley, then ran southwards through a hamlet called Cavrari, then along the eastern side of Unhappy Valley, above the Campiello supply centre, to the escarpment west of the British base at Carriola, by M. Pau. The British forward zone was very narrow as the escarpment was just four miles behind the front line. Cavan immediately deepened the zone by establishing an outpost line well into No Man's Land, which was up to 2kms wide in places.

The sector was thickly forested, mostly mature pine but with some areas of beech saplings. Two roads bisected it. One started in the ruined town of Asiago, entered the sector through the Barental and ran to crossroads at Pria dell'Acqua, then across a large clearing at Granezza to another crossroads (Tattenham Corner), on the edge of the escarpment. From there it wound down the escarpment to foothill villages containing supply depots, plus road and railway routes. The other road ran from the village of Canove (held by the *k.u.k.*), to what the British called Ghelpac Fork, then along a forest track to crossroads (Handley Cross) and on to Carriola, then eastwards along the top of the escarpment to meet roads leading to the plains.

The normal routine was two divisions up on the plateau and one resting on the plains. The divisions on the plateau had two brigades forward and one in reserve. The Corps, and the right division's, headquarters sprawled across the Granezza pasture, along with those of supporting arms and services. The site contained barracks, stores, mule-lines, a smithy, water-points, baths, a disinfection plant, a rifle range, a hospital, a YMCA hut, an Expeditionary Forces Canteen, a cinema-cum-theatre, football pitches, workshops, a refuelling-point for

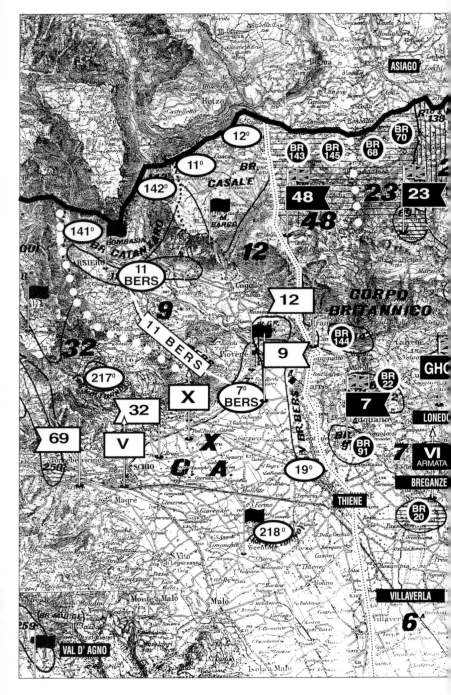

Italian Sixth Army, 1918 Defence Zone, showing British and French sectors.

Panoramic map of British sector, 1918. AZT.

cars and lorries, and of course, a parade ground. (The trolley-bus system linked Granezza to the foothill town of Breganze.) The left division enjoyed similar, but simpler, facilities at Carriola. The reserve division was billeted in a pleasant valley, the Val d'Agno, west of Vicenza, some three days' march from the plateau. British GHQ was at Lonedo, a foothill village about five miles from Granezza. HQ Sixth Army was three miles away in Breganze, while the French HQ was nearby, in the village of Mason di Vicenza.

Defences

These consisted of three lines; the front line skirted the central plain, the second, one kilometre south, ran through the forest along a series of ridges, while the third was close to the escarpment. The front line trenches dated from 1916 and did not meet Western Front standards, as they lacked traverses. They were blown into the

Asiago, 1918. FRANCIS MACKAY

Italian mule train at Granezza. VITTORIO CORA.

limestone, with here and there breastworks built from blocks of rock. The trenches were deep, damp and dangerous as the limestone shattered under artillery or mortar fire, producing razor sharp shards which caused hideous injuries At frequent intervals there were sprigs, short stretches of trench leading to machine-gun or trench mortar emplacements The few dug-outs constructed by the Italians were

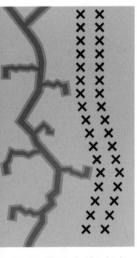

Italian Trench 'Sprigs'

death-traps as, due to the lie of the land, the narrow entrances generally faced in-coming artillery, mortar and machine-gun fire. The dugouts, *'tana di volpe'* (fox-dens), had to be deep to provide strength, as the local rock has an inherent structural weakness, termed by geologists a 'Dolomite Arch.' Front trenches had burrows, variations of *tana di volpe*, leading to observation or machine-gun posts beyond the parapet, and to provide access to the glacis and wire for patrols and working parties. (*Tana di volpe* should be taken here to refer to these burrows.)

The front line generally followed the contours which meant that unless thickly manned, Italian-style, posts were hidden from each other. The wire entanglements (which in some places were surprisingly high, twelve to fifteen feet, because of snow drifts), were considered inadequate by RE experts, who learned the hard way about erecting pickets in limestone. This required use of power-drills then hard (and skilled) work with hammer and mandrel. Tools were in short supply, as were engineers with mining or quarrying experience, so much of the wire was mounted just inside the forests, with trunks or stumps used in place of pickets. Unfortunately trees felled by gunfire easily damaged or bridged the entanglements.

The few switches and strong-points were incomplete, and communication trenches were almost unknown. The prevailing theory held them to be superfluous in woods and useless on open slopes, but that changed after the battle of June 1918. The forest provided excellent cover, which was just as well as the *k.u.k.* studded the forward slopes of the northern mountains with OPs and searchlights, which made fine targets for British gunners, despite being constantly moved at night and camouflaged before first light.

Living conditions on the plateau were poor; log-cabins, lean-tos or damp dugouts, and primitive toilet facilities due to the rocky ground. In 1918 the weather remained bitterly cold and snow fell at Carriola as late as early June, so keeping warm, let alone dry, was a major problem.

But the Allies had one major advantage; they had the sun at their backs for most of the day, while the Austrians had to peer into its rays to see anything moving among the southern woods, even if it was only a pall of dust above a forest road to mark the movement of marching troops, or an ammunition lorry, or the 'goodie' van from the EFC, stuffed with sweet and savoury joys for sale to the frontline soldiers.

Artillery

The rocky ground, steep slopes and scarcity of tracks or roads made the siting of artillery difficult, so many guns were mounted in pits blown out of the rock, or on platforms built up from limestone blocks. The guns had to be manhandled into position, and ammunition and supplies brought up by lorry or GS carts, then brought to the gun positions by pack-mule or manpower. The width of No Man's Land meant that artillery had to be as far forward as possible, so the area just behind the front line was usually crammed with guns, howitzers and mortars. Fortunately for the Allies the enemy was short of ammunition so counter-battery fire was a relatively rare occurrence. Hugh Dalton, later to be the first Labour Chancellor of the Exchecquer, but serving as a Gunner suabaltern, wrote, in *With British Guns in Italy*, that

> British, French and Italian Batteries were all mixed together

The author investigates a dugout entrance, in the Ghepac Fork area, 1998.

in this sector. On our left came first another British Battery, then two French, one in front of the road and one behind it, then another British, then an Italian. On our right, slightly more forward, the Headquarters of an Italian Heavy Artillery Group, in front of them a British and an Italian Battery, one on each side of the road leading past Kaberlaba to the front line. To the right of the Italian Headquarters, across the San Sisto road, was a French Battery, with two Italian Batteries in front of it. To our own right rear was one Italian Battery and two French, and in rear of them, back along the road to Granezza, our own Brigade Headquarters. This mixture was a good arrangement, stimulating friendly rivalry and facilitating liaison and exchange of ideas. Our relations were specially cordial with the Italian Group Headquarters and with one of the French Batteries on our left.

Access

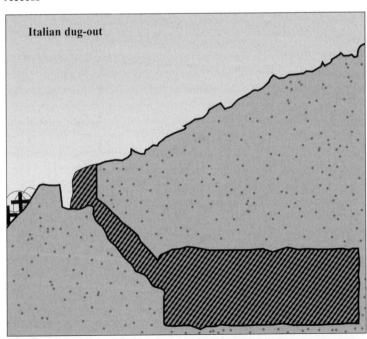

Italian dug-out

Tana di volpe: 'Fox den'.

Vehicles had priority on the escarpment roads so troops travelling to and from the Val d'Agno rest area, or the foothill villages, used *mulaterria*. The British learned from the Italians to allow roughly one hour's march for every thousand feet of altitude, marching for twenty minutes and resting for ten. Lightly equipped troops needed about five hours to ascend from foothill villages such as Calvene or Caltrano. Private Norman Gladden, serving in the Northumberland Fusiliers, in his book *Across The Piave*, scarcely mentions the ascent, so it could not have been too arduous, but described the descent as a joy:

> *It was a beautiful morning with clearer skies than we had seen since our arrival in the mountains. All around us, forming an amphitheatre, were the hills and mountains of the Alpine*

K.u.k. Searchlight and team. Gino Rossato.

Italian 149mm gun position; rock platform. VITTORIO CORA.

British and Italian troops, winter 1917/18, trying to keep warm.
TAYLOR COLLECTION.

fringe, a glorious scene into which we descended with jolting steps but the lightest of hearts, towards the plains stretched below us like an immense carpet, towns and villages, rivers and streams, fields and roads showing up map-like in the brilliant sunshine in a patchwork of a dozen shades of green.

But up or down, it was hard going and the British soldiers did not always appreciate the beauty of the mountains.

Manpower

Flu, mountain fever, struck in May. By early June some units were sending as many as twenty men a day to hospital, while many of those reporting sick were kept in the line on light duties. The two British front line divisions between them had to evacuate 1500 men and in early June had 500 in hospital. As few reinforcements could be spared from the Western Front, manpower was always scarce, and a commander who imperilled his troops by neglect or incompetence could expect short-shrift.

The enemy

On the plateau four Allied corps – Italian XIII and XX, French XII, British XIV (in total eight divisions), faced twelve divisions of the III, XVIII, VI Corps, Eleventh Army, of the Trentino Group of Armies. Each *k.u.k.* division had four regiments, each with three infantry battalions, plus artillery and support units. By June 1918 the two British divisions, with twenty-four battalions, faced the *k.u.k.* 6th and 52nd Divisions (III Corps), and the 38th *Honved* Division (XIII Corps); some thirty-six battalions in total, and an ethnic hotch-potch of German-Austrians, Bosnians, Croats, Czechs, Hungarians, Ruthenes, Slovenes, Slovaks and Tyroleans. After nearly four years of war all were dispirited, weary, hungry, frequently dirty and usually ragged, but still capable of a spirited response if provoked.

After Caporetto the *k.u.k* adopted (and adapted) German infiltration tactics, established training schools and formed *Sturmtruppen* units within each corps. Generally each division had an assault battalion, regiments had an assault company, battalions had an assault platoon while companies had an assault section. In addition there was the Eleventh Army *Sturmbataillon,* a fighting unit but also the instruction battalion for the *Sturmschule* at Levico, in the Val Sugana.

The British discovered an atmosphere of 'live and let live' on the plateau. No Man's Land varied in width from one hundred metres at the Ghelpac Gorge to two thousand metres between Edelweiss Spur, just west of Asiago, and the San Sisto Ridge. It was usually deserted

View of the plains from a muleterria near Tattenham Corner, looking south east

RIVER BRENTA

VENICE

PADU

ADRIATIC SEA

BREGANZE

LONEDO

39

A British soldier views the escarpment without enthusiasm; it was a five hour climb. TAYLOR LIBRARY.

day and night and was so quiet that in early April the Prince of Wales enjoyed a long walk there one morning! Things soon changed. The British quickly dominated No Man's Land, where they built tracks (some metalled), dumped defence stores ready for the offensive, and deployed machine-guns, mortars, and sometimes field guns, there to support trench raids or harass the enemy. The Austrians were more circumspect in their activities, but kept a careful watch on these developments.

Bosnian (Muslim) troops of the Austrian army receiving medals, Val Sugana, 1917. GINO ROSSATO.

Chapter Four

OPERATION RADETZKY
Conrad plays 'va banque'

In spring 1918 the Austrian people and armed forces were weakened and demoralized by the war and other events. The reclusive, ultra-conservative Emperor Franz-Josef died in 1916, having reigned for sixty-eight years. He was succeeded by Karl I, a cavalry officer with strong liberal principles who was bent on taking the lead in political, civil and military affairs. The government, court and population faced a new style of leadership, and not everyone liked it. The new emperor appointed himself *Armeeoberkommandant,* and replaced Conrad with a court favourite, *Generaloberst* Artur Freiherr Arz von Straussenburg. Conrad himself was promoted *Feldmarschal,* received awards and honours - and relegated to the Trentino Group of Armies in his beloved Tyrol, nose-to-nose with the Italians.

Emperor Karl wanted peace and worked diligently to achieve it, but his efforts backfired so badly that in 1918 he received demands from the Kaiser for full economic and military union between Germany and Austria, including calls for troops and artillery for the Western Front. Three options were open to the Austrians on the *Sudwestfront.* First, do nothing; second, retreat from Italy and help the Germans smash the Allies in the west, third, attack. As the Germans were insistent that the *k.u.k.* do *something,* the last was really the only option open if the Empire was to get any more food or other help from Berlin. Unfortunately there was no overall *k.u.k.* commander on the *Sudwestfront* which was divided into two sectors, the western (mountain) one, held by the Trentino Group of Armies, and the eastern one, on the plains, with the Piave Group of Armies commanded by *Feldmarschal* Svetozar Boroevic von Bojna, a tough and resourceful Croat. Both commanders reported to the Emperor.

Conrad, restive in his mountain fastness, planned a master-stroke against the Italians. He dismissed the British and French contingents as

Emperor Karl I.

Austrian offensives, June 1918: Proposed objectives.

insignificant, comparing them to men clinging to a life-raft: *'cut off their hands and they will drown'*. His fertile mind turned again to the Asiago plateau. This, surely, was the real path to victory. Cross it, he reasoned, and the *Welsce* (a sneering name for Italians) would be trapped behind the Piave. He read every document on the terrain and the enemy that his staff could locate, especially reports on the failure of the *Strafexpedition*. One more push then, he thought, would have gained a victory which would have made Caporetto look like a trench-raid. Conrad bombarded Arz with plans - four in all - between January and March. Arz attempted to placate Conrad while denying him supplies and troops as the Emperor did not want more waste of life, and was still hoping to reach an accommodation with the Allies. Boroevic was asked for his views, and for a plan. He recognised the difficulties of a major offensive, especially along the Piave where his forces were at the end of a long and inadequate supply line, and produced a simple plan. Cross the Piave and head for Padua and its supply dumps. Conrad's plan was also simple. Cross the plateau and head for Vicenza and the south. So confident was Conrad of victory that he intended taking along a *Feldmarschal's* baton, to be awarded to the Emperor in Vicenza, or even somewhere further south. Two days to reach Verona, and ten to get to Rome; that was Conrad's vision!

Unfortunately, both plans required not only more forces than each Army Group had at hand, but supplies, transport and war material of all kinds. Decisions were required: to go or stay put, and if the answer was 'go', who had priority? And how were the resources to be allocated? On 11 April Karl summoned Conrad to a conference. Conrad was determined to force a decision from the young Emperor. Boreovic also wanted a decision, and would have been content to make a demonstration along the Piave, to focus the Allies attention there while Conrad swept down from the mountains. Karl reached an ill-fated compromise. Both generals were allocated troops, but not enough for either to meet his needs. They received what supplies were available, but not enough to sustain a long offensive. There were to be two equal offensives, but the objectives of both were too close together so that, even if they were moderately successful, the armies would collide west of Padua.

Zero Day was set for 28 May 1918.

Preparations

Conrad returned to the Trentino Group where his exile had not been wasted. Armies, corps and divisions had been rejuvenated by his energy and optimism. Junior officers and NCOs, not just from the infantry but from *Sappeur* (field engineer) units, were undergoing *Sturmausbildung* (assault training), before returning to their units to conduct local training. Units were rotated out of the line to rest and refit in peaceful valleys, and artillery pieces removed for servicing in the army workshops in and around Trento. Most officers longed to break out of their grim mountain fastness onto the plains, and perhaps attain peace, or at least to achieve another victory over the Italians. Many Austrians believed the offensives would succeed, convinced that infiltration tactics would produce another Caporetto. They forgot that previously they had been used by Germans, and even then not always successfully.

The Trentino Group faced enormous problems and everything seemed to be against them. Late blizzards blocked mountain passes and the supply system nearly collapsed; even when supplies were delivered they were frequently useless. There was a serious shortage of transport; 6,000 draught and pack animals and hundreds of motors were needed, and spares for the few available vehicles. This placed

K.u.k. Sturmtruppen at Mass. FRANCIS MACKAY

greater dependence on 'carrying units', *Trägerabteilung*. Their task was to move supplies the hard way; in backpacks, up *mulaterria* to dumps anything up to 4,000 feet above the depots. But everyone toiled away, for *Befehl ist Befehl*; orders are orders, and traditions died hard in the *k.u.k.*

Reinforcements arrived. Some were *Marschbattalions* composed of raw recruits, recovered wounded, and mutinous ex-PoWs from the *Ostfront* (Russia), others were fully-manned, if unblooded, units of well-fed soldiers dragged reluctantly from comfortable garrisons in the

Tragerabteilung **badge. (Carrying Units)**

homeland. They were directed into side-valleys, far from the plateau, and ensconced in camouflaged huts and caves. Here they settled down to wait. They slept, ate, groused, went to Mass, cracked jokes and lice, played cards - but were told little about the coming offensive, and that they might encounter British and French troops. Conrad received additional artillery, some pieces withdrawn from the farthest reaches of Galicia where the fighting had almost ceased as the Russians pulled out of the war. The guns and their crews moved labouriously into emplacements on the plateau and began, very carefully, to register targets in the Allied defence zone.

The Austrians had to hide troop concentrations, and the busy training areas in the valleys, from reconnaissance aircraft. The Allies had quickly achieved air parity, then air superiority, over much of the front line, and their aircraft roamed more or less at will over the enemy rear areas. The Allies knew about the impending offensive. News came from spies in the Trentino, from military attachés and neutral businessmen in Vienna, from wireless and field-telephone intercepts, air reconnaissance, and above all, from deserters. These included three Czech officers who, accompanied by their servants carrying their portmanteaux, entered the British lines on 12 June and provided information about the forthcoming bombardment and attack. They did not, however, reveal (if they knew) that the British would be attacked; probably they were unwitting pawns of some enterprising *k.u.k* intelligence officers. (On the *Ostfront* Czechs had gone over to the Russians, so few of their compatriots were trusted by 'Austrian' Austrians.) The *k.u.k.* had masked their intentions well, for nearly six divisions were preparing to attack the British sector, from concentration areas in the Val d'Assa, and behind Asiago town.

The Allied air forces carried the war to the enemy, wrecking supply dumps and *Seilbahn* stations. Allied aircraft regularly controlled artillery shoots for heavy and super-heavy railway guns, and bombed and shot-up any target they could find in the valleys or on the mountain slopes, as this mournful *k.u.k.* report reveals:

> *Air fighting greatly increased in liveliness. Whilst at night, when there was good moonlight, both sides did damage with bombs, by day British low-flying fighters* [Sopwith Camels], *in particular, were unpleasantly attentive. Troops in training, railway stations crowded with trains, supply columns unsuspiciously wandering on the road, even single motor cars, were their targets, which often occasioned heavy losses.*

The RAF fighter squadrons established an air interdiction zone over the plateau, seven miles deep and twelve wide, which few Austrian planes penetrated and survived. The Austrians responded to this with 152mm long-range siege guns, which hit the RAF airfield at Villaverla, north of Vicenza, at a range of nearly twenty kilometres. Allied reconnaissance aircraft probed distant valleys, searching for troop concentrations and abnormal rail traffic. But the *k.u.k.* took great care to conceal the heavily laden troop trains and they were not discovered. Assembly areas and forming-up positions in No Man's Land had been reconnoitred, and gaps in the wire carefully widened. Allied action and bad weather forced the Austrians to postpone the offensive for two weeks: Z-Day was now to be Saturday 15 June. Despite this delay, as the clocks ticked off the final hours, fifty artillery batteries were still moving laboriously through torrential rain to the front, and more than two million artillery rounds still lay in dumps and magazines far from the plateau.

The Austrian sense of the romantic showed in the code-names given to the offensives. They reflected the bygone days when the Italians were regularly routed on the Plains of Lombardy. Boroevic's attack was *Operation Albrecht* after the great warrior-prince. Conrad's was named after his idol, that splendid old warrior and bane of the *Welsce, Feldmarschal* Johann Josef Wenzel Anton Franz Karl *Graf* Radetzky von Radetz.

Chapter Five

15/16 JUNE 1918
GRANEZZA
The Battle in the Clouds

The night of 14/15 June 1918 on the Asiago plateau was damp, with a thick mist forming in hollows and valleys. At 3 am precisely Allied observers in mountain-top OPs saw hundreds of signal flares burst into life above the enemy trenches. This was immediately followed by twinkling pin-points of light on the slopes behind as masses of light and medium guns, many dragged forward from the northern valleys during the night, opened fire. Behind the northern ridges sudden flashes revealed the presence of heavier artillery pieces: Operation *Radetzky* had begun.

The Austrian barrage fell mainly on the Allied front line, but signals centres, ammunition dumps and road junctions received attention. The Granezza and Carriola bases were hit, and some shells even whistled over the escarpment to upset staff in the foothill supply dumps. The bombardment lasted for over four hours, and was followed by a massive infantry attack, launched from assembly areas just forward of the Austrian wire. The initial objectives, in the French and British sectors, were Granezza and Carriola, and the edge of the escarpment. On the Allied right the Italian line was breached, and the enemy penetrated about two kilometres towards the escarpment. They were held, but it took five days of bitter fighting to restore the line. In the centre the French beat off a mass attack with only minor casualties. The British were also attacked and the front line breached in several places, but after some hard fighting it was restored.

Radetzky failed, and, after some bitter fighting, so did *Albrecht.* Conrad and Boroevic lost their last battles and the *k.u.k.* lost its will to win.

The British Sector

The Allies knew of Operation *Radetzky,* and were prepared; indeed, they had stood to arms on more than one occasion, ready to repel rumoured attacks which failed to materialize. Possibly some of these false alarms were the result of 'disinformation' spread by ingenious *k.u.k. Propagandastellen,* small teams of experts conducting what are now known as 'psyops' (Psychological Operations). The Allies

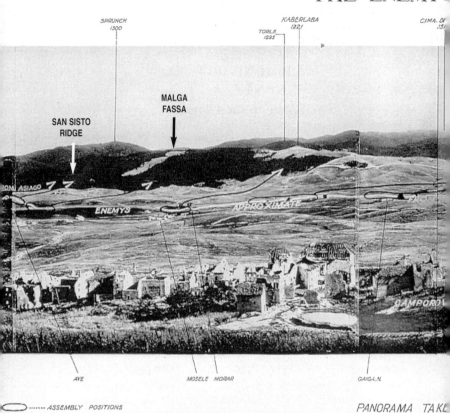

SPRUNCH
1300

KABERLABA
1221

TORLE
1235

CIMA. DI
151

MALGA
FASSA

SAN SISTO
RIDGE

ROM ASIAGO

ENEMYS

APPROXIMATE

FRO

CAMPORI

AVE

MOSELE MORAR

GAIGA.N.

⬭ ·······ASSEMBLY POSITIONS

➡ ·······ROUTES OF ATTACK

PANORAMA TAKE
AS

Austrian objectives in British and French sectors 15 June 1918.

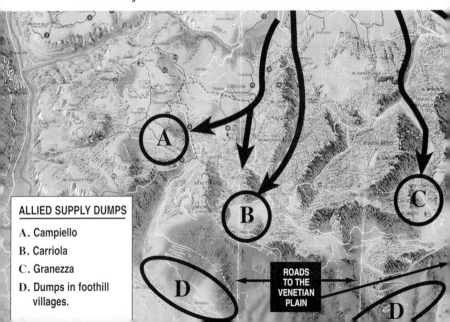

A

B

C

ALLIED SUPPLY DUMPS

A. Campiello

B. Carriola

C. Granezza

D. Dumps in foothill
villages.

D

ROADS
TO THE
VENETIAN
PLAIN

D

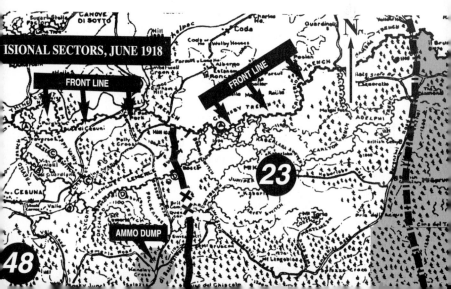

FORAORO 1503   LEMERLE 1234   PAU 1420   SUMMANO 1299   CESUNA   AMBROSINI FO

GHELPAC VALLEY

CROCE   CAMPOROVERE   CANOVE   STELLA

RASTA (1200 METRES)
MY.

INTELLIGENCE, G.H.Q. ITALY

Divisional sectors, June 1918.

ISIONAL SECTORS, JUNE 1918

FRONT LINE   FRONT LINE

N

23

AMMO DUMP

48

BRITISH FRONT LINE DIVISIONS, BRIGADES & INFANTRY BATTALIONS

Note: 1/South Staffs & 21/Manchester, 91 Bde, 7th Division, were on the plateau during the battle but were not engaged by the k.u.k. The remaining battalions of the brigade, 2/Queens & 22/Manchester, were in reserve in villages at the foot of the escarpment, but moved up to the plateau late on 15 June to act as Corps reserve.

 23rd Division

68 Brigade

| 10/Northumberland Fusiliers | 11/Northumberland Fusiliers | 12/Durham Light Infantry | 13/Durham Light Infantry |

69 Brigade

| 11/West Yorkshires | 8/Green Howards | 9/Green Howards | 10/Duke of Wellington's |

70 Brigade

| 11/Sherwood Foresters | 8/KOYLI | 8/York & Lancs | 9/York & Lancs |

9/South Staffordshires (Pioneer battalion)

 48th Division

143 Brigade

| 1/5 R Warwicks | 1/6 R Warwicks | 1/7 R Warwicks | 1/8 R Warwicks |

144 Brigade

| 1/4 Gloucesters | 1/6 Gloucesters | 1/7 Worcesters | 1/8 Worcesters |

145 Brigade

| 1/5 Gloucesters | 1/4 Ox & Bucks LI | 1/1 Bucks Bn | 1/4 Royal Berks |

5th (Cinque Ports) Bn Royal Sussex (Pioneer battalion)

Battle of Asiago - 15/16 June 1918
K.U.K. FORMATIONS FACING THE BRITISH CORP

Note: 1. *In 1918 Infanterieregimenten had three battalions*
2. *Only units shown in* **bold** *were in contact with the British*
3. *The names below some regiments are 'hereditary' titles.*

Eleventh Army

General Victor Graf Scheuchenstuel

III Corps

Generaloberst Hugo Mariny von Malastow

Only three of the four divisions appear to have engaged the British. Elements of the 28th Division may have been encountered when British patrols tried to enter the k.u.k. *lines in force late on 16 June*

6 Cavalry Division
(dismounted)

Hussar Regiment	8 Dragoon Regt	11 Dragoon Regt	15 Dragoon Regt
rzog Franz Salvator	*Graf Montecuccoli*	*K.u.K. Franz Josef I*	*Erzherzog Josef August*

6 Division

17	**27 IR**	**81 IR**	**127 IR**
nterie Regiment			*Freiherr von Waldstatten*

52 Division

6 B-H	**26 IR**	**42 IR**	**74 IR**
(Bosnian)	**Schreiber**		*Freiherr von Schonaich*

28 Division

6 B-H	11 IR	**28 IR**	47 IR
nterie Regiment			

XIII Corps

General Friedrich Csanady von Bekes
5 Division

16 Division

2 IR	**31 IR**	**52 IR**	**138 IR**
	Pucheria	**Erzherzog Friedrich**	
	1/61 Sappeur **Battalion**		

38 *Honved* Division

1 Honved IR	**22 Honved IR**	**23 Honved IR**	**24 Honved IR**
	3/61 Sappeur **Battalion**		

42 *Honved* Division

5 Honved IR	**26 Honved IR**	27 Honved IR	**28 Honved IR**

believed, or had been led to believe, that the Austrians would attack only the Italian and the French, and that British positions would be bombarded but not assaulted. But, as a precaution, the British divisions were instructed to continue with preparations for a forthcoming Allied offensive, but to remain on the alert to defend their positions. (The Allied offensive was due to start on 18 June, and was to be a spoiling attack intended to disrupt preparations for *Radetzky*.) On 12 June the British divisions instructed their brigades to have all units at immediate readiness to man their battle positions, with reconnaissance patrols closely watching the front and wire-watching patrols searching for signs of enemy wire-cutting parties or reconnaissance teams, and to ensure that precautions against gas were observed. Close liaison was to be maintained with the French on the right flank. The Italian position on the left flank was virtually impregnable, protected as it was by the deep gorges of the Ghelpac and the Val d'Assa.

The 23rd Division was on the right (Granezza) flank; the 48th on the left (Carriola). Most of the 7th Division was resting in the Val d'Agno, three days march away, but it's divisional artillery, and two infantry battalions, were on the plateau, ready to support the Allied offensive. British preparations included creating a huge artillery ammunition dump at Handley Cross, an important cross-roads in the Carriola sector.

The French XII Corps (General Jean Graziani, French despite his Italian name) had the 23e and 24e Divisions on the plateau. The former occupied the front line, covering a front of 3,300 metres. When *k.u.k.* plans became known, General Graziani had the division close up to the right, and insinuated three battalions of the 24e Division, one each from the 50e, 108e and 126e *Regiments d'Infantrie,* into the left flank as he recognised that the Barental Road would be a key enemy objective.

The Right Flank

The 23rd Division (Major-General Sir James Babington), covering a front of about 5,500 metres, had 68 and 70 Brigades in the front line and 69 Brigade in reserve. The situation facing the division was complicated. It was holding the line in preparation for the Allied offensive. On 17 June the battalions leading the British assault were intended to relieve the front line battalions which would retire to reserve positions. When the offensive started the extreme right front section of the line would be occupied by French units after the attacking battalions had left the trenches. Yet at the same time the

Asiago Plateau, southern hills: area defended by French (foreground) and British (forest, as far as left horizon - wooded ridge). VITTORIO CORA.

division had to prepare for a heavy enemy bombardment, if not an attack. In view of this, and in accordance with current defence doctrine, the front line was only lightly manned. Unfortunately all battalions were seriously under-strength, so the front line was very lightly manned indeed. Apart from the ravages of `flu, many officers, NCOs and men were absent on leave or attending courses; (the two divisional Machine Gun battalions had fifty infantrymen attached for instruction during the period 1-14 June).

During the battle the division was attacked by elements of three

23rd Division sectors, June 1918, with brigade operational areas.

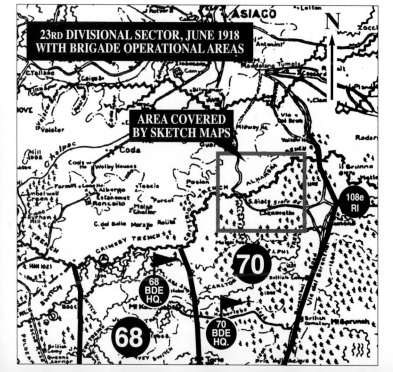

k.u.k. divisions, the 6th, 16th and the 38th *Honved* (Hungarian). The attackers included men from the 21, 22, 24 *Honved*, and part of the 6th Austrian, infantry regiments, about thirteen battalions in all, and some assault engineers from the 61st *Sappeur* battalion. The front line was manned by five British battalions. It was briefly breached in two places but the *k.u.k* attackers were quickly evicted and suffered horrendous losses.

70 Brigade

The brigade (Brigadier-General L.H. Gorden), covered about 3,000 metres of front with two battalions each with two companies forward. Brigade headquarters lay in the support line, south east of M. Kaberlaba.

The right front battalion, holding the San Sisto Ridge, was 11/Sherwood Foresters, 'The Men from the Greenwood', (Lieutenant-Colonel CE Hudson, DSO MC), with a frontage of about 1,000 metres. The actual length of the front (Alhambra) trench was closer to 1,800 metres. Any attack would probably come from the Austrian strong-points at Sec (Sech on some maps), Villa Dal Brun and Ave.

The left front battalion was the 9/York and Lancasters, covering around 800 metres of front, (Criterion Trench - probably 1,200 metres long), ending almost opposite Poslen farmstead. Any attack would probably come from the direction of the dead ground north of the ruined farm at Guardinalti. The battalion had two companies in the front line and one in support, in Malga Fassa Switch near a large clearing in the forest on the north slope of Prinele ridge above a glen, see panorama. The fourth company was even further uphill, in Carlton

Air oblique Asiago and San Sisto ridge, looking south.

SAN SISTO RIDGE

VILL DAL BRUN

SEC

ASIAGO

Trench, and Huddersfield, Harrogate and Ilkley redoubts.

In support was the 8/Y&L with three companies in the western part of Adelphi Trench, and one in a 'fort' guarding the top of the Malga Fassa Switch. The reserve battalion was 8/KOYLI, in the woods near Pria dell'Acqua, with (in accordance with the divisional defence plan) one company, in this case 'A', at the disposal of the right forward battalion during an attack.

In the days before the Austrian attack these battalions had been busy. Defences had been strengthened, arcs of fire agreed and marked, and counter-attacks 'walked through' by company commanders and senior NCOs, then by junior officers and NCOs, then, when possible, by complete platoons or sections.

San Sisto Ridge

This ridge was the key to the centre of the Allied front. If it fell the British and French front lines would be outflanked. It is a tadpole-shaped mound 1,000 metres long rising some 60 metres above the plain. Between it and the town of Asiago are meadows, rocky hummocks and a low ridge, running from Villa Dal Brun to Guardinalti and Poslen, and scattered farms and houses, which in 1918 were ruins turned into redoubts by the Austrians.

The ridge was covered in pine-woods and light undergrowth. The steep southern slope of the San Sisto ridge contained several deep, damp and dangerous Italian dug-outs. At the bottom of this slope, in San Sisto Valley, was a long clearing containing a stretch of pasture, and a track. At the western end was a small chapel which was used as a dressing station by the Sherwood Forester's medical officer and

Ground to north of San Sisto Ridge, looking north east. FRANCIS MACKAY.

stretcher-bearers during the battle. The clearing was pitted with gun and mortar pits, and their associated trenches and ammunition bays. Rude huts were scattered under the trees, and shelters rigged against banks and from fallen trees. Latrines had been erected at various points, and hard-standings laid for mule and horse lines. At a discrete distance from the mules and latrines a couple of cooking areas had been built near the stub of an Italian pipe-line. (Earlier, this had been an Italian field kitchen, serving units in the northern mountains; by the time the pasta got to them, it was said, it was so congealed that only a sharp bayonet would cut it.)

The wooded northern slope fell away gradually to merge into pasture land. The front line, Alhambra Trench, lay about thirty metres back from forest edge. The trenches were of the old Italian design, blown from rock, lacking traverses but with some stubs leading to machine-gun pits, and few dugouts. The trenches were protected by a belt of wire set entirely within the forest. Some rudimentary belts ran diagonally up the ridge to form switches. (The remnants of the entanglements can still be found in the thin undergrowth.) A second trench ran along the top of the ridge, some three hundred metres or so behind the front line and connected to it by a couple of communication trenches. This line was a mix of blown and built-up trenches; and there were several dugouts, pits for support weapons and some *tana di volpe*, many still in existence and easily found.

South of the clearing is a hogback, Prinele Ridge, considerably higher than San Sisto Ridge. Adelphi Trench ran diagonally across this

Cross-section: San Sisto Ridge, not to scale.

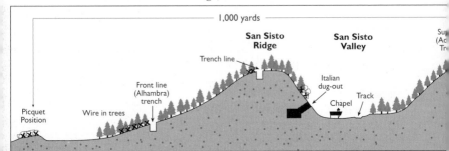

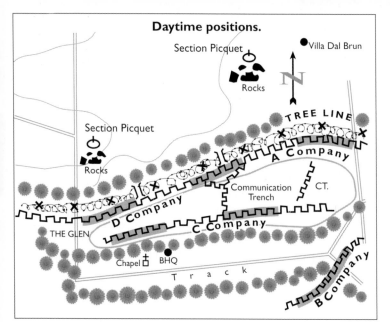

Daytime positions.

Section Picquet

Villa Dal Brun

Rocks

N

Section Picquet

TREE LINE

A Company

Rocks

Communication Trench

CT.

D Company

C Company

THE GLEN

Chapel † BHQ

B Company

T r a c k

11/Sherwood Foresters, San Sisto Ridge. Time 6pm 14 June 1918.

slope from Malga Fassa Fort down to the eastern end of the clearing and into the French sector. Triangle Track connected the San Sisto valley to Pria dell'Acqua.

11/Sherwood Foresters

The Battalion occupied the San Sisto feature on 11 June, after a period in reserve. It was under-strength: only 19 out of 34 officers were in the line, while the two forward companies, A and D, each had less than a hundred all ranks to man around 900 metres of trench, and provide a platoon for night picquet and outpost duty. D Company was commanded by Captain EA Frith and A Company by Captain EH Brittain MC.

Captain Edward Harold Brittain was the adored elder brother of Vera Brittain. When war broke out the Brittain family had been living in Buxton and Edward sought a commission in the county regiment. He joined the 11/Sherwood Foresters in France, was wounded on the first day of the Somme, and awarded the MC. In 1914 Vera had been

San Sisto valley, pasture and chapel, looking west towards the glen.
FRANCIS MACKAY

an undergraduate at Oxford but became a VAD Nurse after her fiancée, Roland Leighton, was mortally wounded with the 1/7 Worcesters at Hébuterne in December 1915. After the war she wrote *Testament of Youth,* married and was the mother of former Labour Cabinet Minister Baroness Shirley Williams.

When, on 11 June 1918, A Company slithered down through the woods and into the front line trench to take over from B Company 8/Y&L, it mustered less than one hundred all ranks. There were only three officers, Captain Brittain, Lieutenant Andrew Swale and Second-Lieutenant Coleman Sallmeyer; the 2i/c and the other subalterns were attending training courses. After settling-in, the officers made contact with the French on their right, a company of the 2e Battalion, 108e RI, whose company commander, Lieutenant Gautier, proved helpful and co-operative. A Company also established contact with D Company, and with C Company, in support in the ridge-top trench. This company had only four weak platoons to cover about nine hundred metres of trench, so inevitably there were wide gaps. B Company was in reserve, in Adelphi Trench, close to the track leading from the clearing southwards to the Barental Road. The company was in touch with the French, via a jointly manned liaison post next to the Barental Road, and with the 8/Y&L on the left, in the upper reaches of Adelphi Trench.

Battle Headquarters, consisting of the Commanding Officer; the Adjutant, Captain EW Bird; the Intelligence Officer, Second-Lieutenant T Hodson; and some signallers and runners plus Sergeant W Ellis DCM MM, of B Coy, were in the clearing, near the chapel. A Echelon, under the command of the 2i/c, Major NH Young DSO (Royal Inniskilling Fusiliers, attached), was located right rear, near B Company. B Echelon, the Quartermaster and his staff, and the RSM in charge of the first-line ammunition reserve, ready to re-supply the battalion, was at Granezza.

Supporting units

A number of other units were in the immediate area, including four Vickers teams from B Company, 23rd Battalion MGC. This unit had several reserve positions on the ridge, surveyed, sign-posted and ready for use, whatever transpired. The 70th Light Trench Mortar Battery had six guns in the area, two on the ridge and four covering the front line from positions at the edge of the clearing. The 23rd Trench Mortar Battery RFA had surveyed the ridge and established sites for 6-inch Newton Mobile Mortars, including one in No Man's Land, ready to support a night raid on Ave. This site was visited by the Divisional

Trench Mortar Officer and an instructor from the GHQ Trench Mortar School at Tezze Padovana who, as recorded in the Battery War Diary, 'visited S Sisto and walked out to see the site for the section forward. Had tea at Battn headquarters.' Also in the immediate area was the Right Group, 102 Brigade, RFA. The 18-pdrs of B and D Batteries, with range tables and plotting boards marked up, and ammunition stacked ready for the Allied offensive, were in the clearing. An Italian trench mortar unit, the 268o *Batterie Bombarde,* 114o *Gruppo,* Italian Artillery, commanded by *Maggiore* Mario Van Den Heuval, an Italian despite his Dutch name, occupied pits in the woods to the south of the clearing. The whole area was therefore crammed with men, weapons, ammunition, supplies, carts, limbers, and mules, a marvellous target for a strafe by *k.u.k.* gunners, who had the area precisely plotted as their infantry had reached it during the *Strafexpedition* under cover of a heavy barrage.

Layered defence

At last light on Friday 14 June, platoons of British infantry, one from each company in the front line, climbed from their trenches and moved cautiously through patrol lanes in the wire, past sentries who then replaced barbed-wire knife-rest 'gates' into the gaps. These platoons were the night picquets, who occupied prominent features in No Man's Land, then established outposts close to the enemy positions, watching and listening for any threatening movement. The outposts were the outer layer of the British defences; the picquets the second. Their task was to delay an enemy advance, then fall back on the next layer, the 'machine-gun line', forward of the wire and covering the approaches to the main position. Both the picquets and the Vickers teams were under strict instructions to withdraw through the wire only if threatened with encirclement.

Once the outposts had been manned, the Sherwood Forester's picquets consisted of little more than ten men. The right-hand one, (Second-Lieutenant Sallmeyer), occupied a lightly-wired position on a rocky mound west of the Villa Dal Brun, watching the approach from Sec, with outposts about a hundred and fifty metres or so nearer the enemy wire. The right Vickers post (guns R1 and R2) covered approaches from Sec and Ave South. D Company picquet (Second-Lieutenant Cheetham) occupied a rocky mound beside the track to Ave South, with outposts near the ruins of Guardinalti. In the Vickers post gun R3 covered the front of the ridge, and R4 the forest edge towards the ruined farm at Poslen.

First shots

Throughout the night of 14 June Allied Artillery bombarded enemy cross-roads, suspected forming-up positions and assembly areas. They fired short barrages at 11.45 pm and 2.45 am, which disrupted the *k.u.k.* assault groups moving into assembly areas. In the Allied trenches 'stand-to' was ordered at 11.30 pm in readiness for yet another rumoured night attack, but nothing happened, other than more sleep lost by weary troops. The weather was showery and a thick mist covered the plain and filled the valleys between the southern hills. Miserable weather, but a relief after days of heavy rain. At 2.45 am Hugh Daltons' howitzer, No 3 (of 464th Siege Battery, RGA), was tasked at short notice to fire, 'at his leisure', ten rounds of HE at an Austrian searchlight on M. Moscaigh, north of Asiago. At 3 am, just as hill-top observers detected the first glimmerings of dawn, the Austrian

11/Sherwood Foresters, San Sisto Ridge. Midnight 14/15 June 1918. Refer to map, page 53.

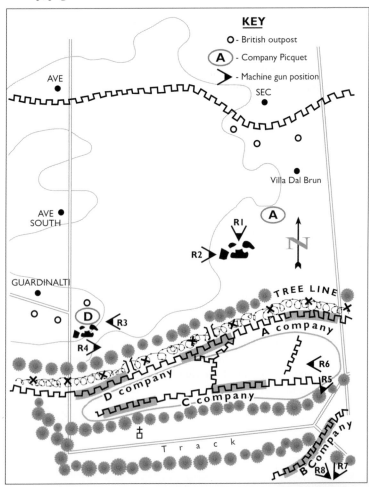

artillery burst into action, and for four hours rained shells and mortar bombs onto the front line. Every type of gun, howitzer and mortar was employed, firing all types of ammunition - HE, shrapnel, gas, even some 305 mm armour-piercing shells, left in a magazine after bombardments on the steel cupolas of Italian frontier forts. The barrage was intense, but considered by Allied staff officers to be dispersed (HE shells interspersed with gas ones; the blast dispersed the fumes) uncoordinated, inaccurate and lacking in volume. Be that as it may, it destroyed trenches, cut telephone lines and hit the Handley Cross ammunition dump, which caught fire and exploded, rendering the adjacent cross-roads impassable for hours. It also destroyed, among many other things, the signal circuits at the crossroads, and made their repair almost impossible. The barrage also damaged the wire at many points on the front, and falling trees formed handy bridges over the entanglements for the enemy.

At 3.20 am Corps HQ ordered the outposts in, fortunately before the signals network was disrupted. On the San Sisto ridge the barrage rapidly put the power-buzzers and telephone lines out of action, and blocked tracks from the rear with fallen trees. The volume of gas sent over was so great that at one stage the vapours were literally pouring down both sides of the ridge and flooding the clearing. Trees were set on fire and the smell of the burning wood made gas difficult to detect, so that masks had to be worn at all times. The Foresters began to suffer casualties and the right hand trench mortar and R2 Vickers gun were destroyed. A Company suffered numerous casualties by enfilading artillery fire from the village of Gallio and the front line trench was partly wrecked, making movement and control difficult for Captain Brittain. At around 4 am the gas shelling stopped, but the HE and shrapnel fire increased. The rear areas were being shelled and at Granezza two battalions of 69 Brigade were sent to 'gas positions' one hundred metres up in the hills above the camp, where they stayed for some hours before it was considered safe for them to descend. The headquarters huts of the CRA and CRE were wrecked, but there were few casualties. At 5.15 am the enemy barrage slackened but at 5.45 am quickened again. In the meantime, Austrian aircraft had appeared over the central plain but Allied offensive counter-air patrols intercepted them and shot eight down before 5.30 am, thereby preventing damage to Allied rear areas from close-air support missions.

The *k.u.k.* attack from Ave and Sec

At 6.45 am the picquets saw movement to their front as enemy infantry began to emerge from the wire in front of Ave and Sec and adopt assault formations. This was immediately reported (by runner) to the front line companies (and battalion headquarters) and stand-to was ordered. The British artillery did not come into action until after the attack started due to disruption to communications, and ambiguous orders. This was a major factor in the initial successes achieved by the Austrians. Several British accounts of the battle mention this, and how puzzled the front line commanders and soldiers were by the lack of artillery support.

The *k.u.k.* attack was launched by battalions advancing on a two-company front, as best they could, having to debouch from relatively small gaps in their wire and adopt assault formations under fire (albeit limited) from Allied artillery, and machine guns firing SOS missions on fixed lines. There was no ambiguity in their orders. The assault was led by small (six or seven man) *Sturmtruppe* teams armed with flame-throwers, Bangalore torpedoes and machine guns, or carrying shears for wire-cutting, and advancing in what one Battle Narrative described as 'worms'. Their role was to breach wire and other obstacles and break into the front trench. They were followed by *Aufraumungstruppe,* organized into groups of ten to fifteen which spread along trenches, clearing them of defenders with grenades, rifle fire and bayonets or improvised trench-warfare weapons such as sharpened spades, knobkerries and knives. The clearing teams were followed by the *Infanteriewelle,* 'infantry wave', to consolidate and hold the captured lines. They in turn were followed by *Materialtruppen,* carrying parties laden with ammunition, grenades, wire, pickets, water cans and supplies. Once the trench was secure, the *Sturmtruppen* withdrew to their own lines, leaving the infantry to hold off any counter-attacks.

The picquet lines

The picquets only had time to note the approximate numbers and disposition of their assailants, and that they were led by mounted officers, before opening rifle and Lewis gun fire on them. British artillery and trench units at San Sisto also opened fire. The enemy went to ground and, while some returned fire, others enfiladed the picquets, who withdrew to the machine-gun line, and continued to engage the enemy. Unfortunately some of the mortar barrage fell on the right Vickers post, wounding Second Lieutenant Sallmayer and some of the machine gunners. The remaining right-hand gun (R1) fired four complete belts, 1,000 rounds, delaying the advance and inflicting numerous casualties on the enemy. The post now being outflanked and bombed, the machine-gunners only stayed long enough to provide covering fire as the picquet ran back through the patrol lane in the wire and into the trenches. The machine-gunners then withdrew through the wire, re-mounted their gun and re-engaged the enemy. The machine-gunners were surprised to find that an infantry section behind them did not join in, for reasons unknown. After twenty minutes the Vickers team was forced to withdraw again, and went to re-inforce another post on the ridge, containing R7 and R8 gun teams.

In the left Vickers post, R4 gun team engaged a large assault force swarming over the Poslen-Guardinalti ridge, inflicting heavy casualties and wearing out the gun's barrel in the process. This was replaced in quick time, and firing continued by both guns, but at 8 am the post was almost surrounded by enemy advancing through dead ground unmasked by the withdrawal of the R2 gun. The machine-gunners retired through the wire into prepared fire positions on the ridge and continued to engage the enemy forces crossing the ridge. The two guns fired over 10,000 rounds in the course of the day, and inflicted serious casualties on the enemy.

The front line breached

Some *k.u.k* troops followed the withdrawing Vickers teams towards, and into, the tree-line. However, they were held up by the wire and by heavy fire from the defenders. It was now 7.15 am. The enemy took cover and started to crawl forward to the wire. (The Forester's War

Picquets and M/G posts driven in, line breached.

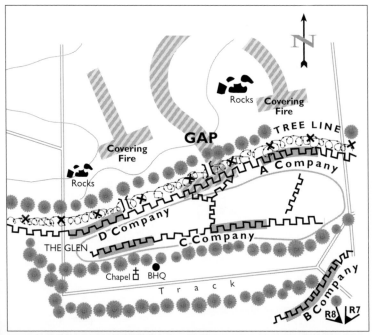

Diary records that *Flammenwerfer* were used against the front line but at too great a range to be effective.) The enemy then got through the wire, either by crossing it on fallen trees, through gaps cut by shrapnel, Bangalore torpedoes, *Sturmtruppen* shears – or by a patrol gap left open by withdrawing troops. The enemy not only got through the wire but into the front line and started to clear the trench, working right and left from the point of entry. One clearing group worked its way west towards the positions held by D Company, but were halted after about a hundred metres. The other group worked eastwards, forcing the few defenders from A Company to withdraw. A breach of some two hundred metres was made in the British front line, and rapidly began to fill with the enemy. More were working through the wire or providing covering fire to keep the defenders heads down. Both A and D Companies reacted by attempting to block the enemy clearing parties, and forming defensive flanks, despite their limited numbers and the need to suppress the fire of the enemy outside the wire.

The death of Edward Brittain

A Company had suffered severe casualties from artillery fire and was trying to hold nearly eight hundred metres of the line with (probably) only fifty rifles; an impossible task even when they were reinforced by the picquet platoon. Brittain, by now apparently the only unwounded officer in the company, appeared on the scene, returning from consulting with the French. Rapidly organizing a counter-attack group, which included some French soldiers, he led an attack which forced the enemy back. Some jumped out of the trench and ran back towards others coming through the wire. These enemy troops went to ground and opened fire on the Foresters, as did machine-gunners and riflemen on both sides of the wire. Brittain re-organized the defence of the trench, forming a flank with what troops were available. He

Breach sealed, Captain Brittain killed.

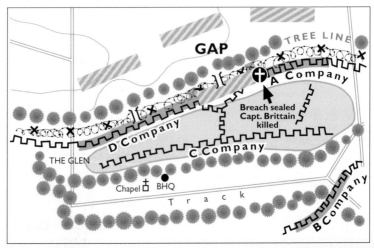

apparently paused to observe the enemy, and was killed, possibly sniped by an Austrian officer.

His death was not more poignant than that of any other young officer or soldier but the eloquence of his sister's writing ensured that the anguish felt by his family and friends was recorded for future generations. She articulated for others not so gifted with words the agony of yet another death among those nearest and dearest to a family. After many years, *Testament of Youth* still has the capacity to move, as many of to-day's generation will testify.

Captain EH Brittain MC.
Sherwood Foresters Collection.

One curious aspect of the *k.u.k.* attack, and of the initially successful breach of the British wire, was the apparent failure of the *Sturmtruppen* to find another way through or over the entanglements. Also, the successful breach appears to have been made almost exactly at the juncture of the two companies. Possibly this was the result of good luck in finding a gap, or of exploiting a patrol lane, or of good reconnaissance. The mere fact that the British rarely saw or met enemy patrols in No Man's Land did not mean they were not conducted, only that none were seen.

The ridge-top attacked

When Brittain was killed the Austrians had at least ten machine-gun teams inside the British wire, and attackers poured into the breach until more than two hundred were jammed into a small space. About thirty charged up a communication trench to the top of the ridge and poured into an undefended stretch of trench between two of C Company's positions. A message from D Company containing news of the breach reached Lieutenant-Colonel Hudson at 8 am - and was immediately confirmed when some of the enemy reached the edge of the ridge and opened fire on the Battle Headquarters group.

Hudson was young, twenty-six, and he did not lack courage, nor was he indecisive. He had risen from Sandhurst cadet (admittedly a mature one) to lieutenant-colonel commanding an infantry battalion in less than four years. He now acted with speed, decisiveness and bravery. Instantly realizing the gravity of the situation he led the headquarters group across the road and into the woods. At all times the group was under heavy small-arms fire at very close range. It was also under shell fire as the enemy barrage had lifted from the front line once the *Sturmtruppen* in the British wire had indicated, by signal flares, that they were close to the front line trench. Once in the woods,

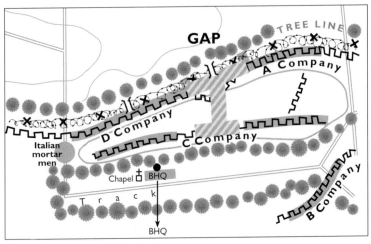

Austrians gain ridge top trench.

Hudson found the Italian mortar gunners and *Maggiore* Van Den Heuval, who realized an emergency had occurred and was eager to help. Hudson quickly organized a counter-attack force from his command group and about a dozen or so Italians. While this party, under the eye of Sgt Ellis, loaded their weapons, sorted out their kit and checked bayonets and grenades, Hudson ordered two platoons from B Company forward to secure the ridge, along with a platoon from the 8/KOYLI company in direct support, waiting near Pria dell'Acqua. He despatched messages to Major Young, advising him that the front line was broken and that a counter-attack was being mounted. This information was also sent to Brigade Headquarters.

The *Maggiore* and about fifty of his mortarmen were sent to the small glen at the western end of the ridge to cover the gap between the Foresters and the 9/Y&L. The Italians also provided local protection for Vickers R10, 15 and 16, and for the left flank of D Company, allowing them to concentrate on holding the front line and maintaining their right defensive flank.

Hudson's counter-attack

Hudson now led the scratch force of British orderlies, batmen, runners and Italian mortar men out of the woods, across the road and up the side of the ridge in a desperate counter-attack. They succeeded, against all the odds. They charged straight at the enemy, firing revolvers and rifles, and throwing grenades into the trench. Some of the enemy were wounded, others surrendered and the remainder retreated rapidly down the slope, leaving behind twenty prisoners and some machine guns and *Flammenwerfer*. The prisoners were searched and interrogated. One wounded enemy officer revealed that his unit

66

had been brought straight to the start-line from a distant holding area and had not been briefed on any aspect of the attack! He added that the unit had been told it would face trifling opposition and only the last stage of the attack would be arduous.

The reinforcing platoons from B Company were delayed by the enemy barrage When they arrived at the ridge they were used to form defensive flanks, as it was thought the Battalion had been cut-off. They were then joined by the 8/KOYLI platoon before all were recalled to the centre and re-deployed. Hudson, having ensured the top of the ridge was adequately garrisoned, sent a message by runner to Brigade Headquarters stating that the ridge-top had been secured and that he was proceeding to re-establish the front line. He would have been told by the French Liaison Officer that the 108e RI battalion on the right of A Company had been re-inforced by three companies, two from the 126e RI and one from the 115e RI, and therefore that flank was secure. Hudson then moved downhill towards D Company, accompanied by Sergeant Ellis and three of the headquarters group, probably including Privates R Springall and HF Groom, both from B Company and decorated for their conduct in the battle. When this party arrived at the front line they found troops of D Company advancing along it to try and locate the enemy. Just as the CO arrived someone spotted an Austrian sentry lying about twenty yards in front of what appeared to be the limit of the enemy-held section of the trench: he was stalked and captured. Hudson and Sergeant Ellis then continued to advance. They suddenly caught sight of *k.u.k.* uniforms and helmets in the trench to their front, and, in the words of the Battalion history:

> *Sergeant Ellis, excited by the prospect of further captures, rushed forward, but immediately seeing the whole trench filled with the enemy, turned and jumped back into our line, running*

Lieutenant Colonel Hudson's counter attack. Italian mortarmen were to hold 'Glen'.

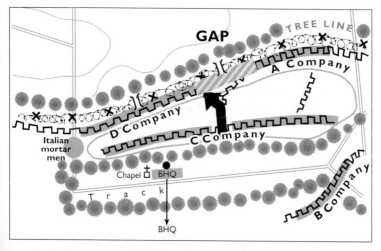

back out of view of Colonel Hudson. The latter, not realizing the sergeant had escaped, rushed forward firing on the enemy and calling on them to surrender. The hands along the trench went up, and an Austrian officer was singled out and came forward covered by Colonel Hudson's revolver. Here one of the enemy, unnoticed, threw a bomb killing his own officer and severely wounding Colonel Hudson who, unable to rise, rolled back to the cover of a communication trench and fell in. The enemy allowed him to go without firing. However, the exact position of the enemy was known. Colonel Hudson, although severely wounded in the right foot and leg, prepared the dispositions for the counter attack.

Lieutenant Colo[nel] CE Hudson VC, and Bar, MC.
Sherwood Foresters Collecti[on]

Hudson also ordered a message be sent to Major Young advising him of the situation and handing over command of the Battalion. Some men from D Company reached the colonel and rendered first-aid before removing him. It was now about 9.30 am. At company headquarters Hudson instructed the D Company commander to await reinforcements before mounting the counter-attack.

Second attack from Sec

A further threat to the ridge materialized when an enemy force emerged from Sec and advanced along the main road in closely bunched assault formations. They were engaged by British and French machine guns and artillery, and scattered. Many took cover while others retreated to their start line by the wire or fell, killed or wounded. However, their officers and senior NCOs rallied them and again they advanced, this time in extended order. Once more they were engaged with machine-gun fire, and at 10 am this attack had been broken for good.

Brigade Headquarters, on receiving the message from Young, had ordered 8/KOYLI to send the remainder of the company at Pria dell'Acqua forward to San Sisto; and to replace it with another company to act as a road block if the enemy broke through the front line in force. The 8/Y&L sent a carrying party of thirty men with SAA and grenades to the Foresters, and four Vickers guns from the divisional reserve were deployed on the right flank of the ridge.

Clearing the breach

Back at San Sisto, Young ensured all was secure. This included checking the disposition of the seven platoons in the ridge-top trench, liaising with the support weapons teams, and with the Italian mortar men holding the western end. A Company, 8/KOYLI, arrived at about 12.30 pm and Young directed the company commander, Captain BW Horsley MC, to send two platoons onto the ridge and the remainder to D Company to help clear the front line trench and make contact with A Company and the French. About 180 Austrians now occupied about three hundred metres of the British front line, and had mounted machine-guns on the parapets. The intruders were in constant contact with colleagues on both sides of the wire who were providing covering fire. In view of the number of enemy machine guns inside and outside the trench, the two company commanders decided to counter-attack with the KOYLI group by bombing along it rather than launching a frontal attack. Horsley organized the platoons into three groups: fire-support, bombing and follow-up. By about 2.30 pm the front line had been restored.

Follow-up

The bag of *k.u.k.* men and material was impressive, 300 bodies were counted in No Man's Land in front of the ridge and four officers and 150 ORs were captured. Also captured were eight machine-guns, five *Flammenwerfer,* one trench mortar and many rifles; dozens of grenades, machine-gun tripods, water cans, pipes and buckets, spare-parts wallets and replacement barrels, and hundreds of rounds of ammunition. The rest of the battle was, for the Sherwood Foresters, comparatively quiet. The enemy attack drifted westwards, so the guns in the valley behind the ridge, the Vickers guns and trench mortars on its sides and top, and nearby howitzers, continued firing at targets of opportunity on the plain. This was thick with hurrying *k.u.k.* gun batteries, some moving forward and others wheeling into position. Forward Observations Officers and their orderlies set up OPs,

Austrians expelled, ridge top held in strength.

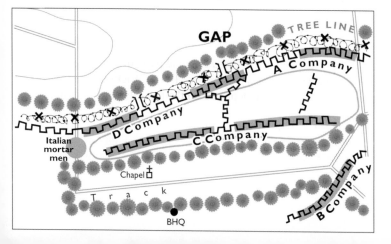

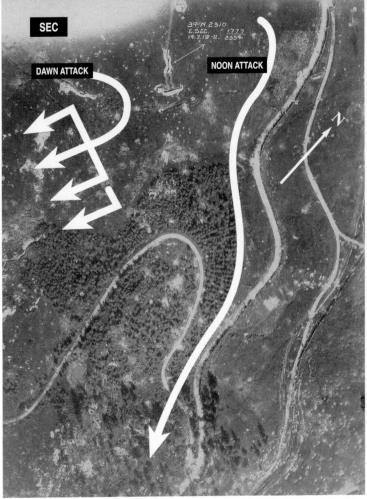

Sec *k.u.k.* **redoubt – start point for two attacks on the British, 15 June 1918.** Worcestershire Collection.

unreeling telephone cables or setting up signalling stations. Medical teams were in constant action, tending the wounded, lifting them onto stretchers and carrying them a long and dangerous journey back to the safety of their front line. The slaughter caused by the Allied artillery was immense, and effectively destroyed the Austrian follow-up forces to such an extent that even if the British line had been seriously breached it is unlikely they could have sustained the momentum of the attack beyond the reserve positions.

Aftermath

Hudson, VC, DSO and Bar, MC, Captain (Temporary Lieutenant-Colonel) Charles Edward: 11th Battalion The Sherwood Foresters

Victoria Cross - London Gazette - 11.7.1918:

For most conspicuous bravery and devotion to duty when his battalion was holding the right front sector during an attack on the British front, at San Sisto Ridge near Asiago, Italy, on 15.6. 1918. The shelling had been very heavy on the right, the trench destroyed, and considerable casualties had been incurred, and all the officers on the spot were killed or wounded. This enabled the enemy to penetrate our front line. The enemy pushed the advance as far as the support line which was the key to the right flank. The situation demanded immediate action. Lieut Col Hudson, recognizing its gravity, at once collected various headquarters details, such as orderlies, servants, runners, etc., and together with some allies, personally led them up the hill. Driving the enemy down the hill towards our front line, he again led a party of about five up the trench, where there were about 200 enemy, in order to attack them from the flank. He then, with two men, got out of the trench and rushed the position, shouting to the enemy to surrender, some of whom did. He was then severely wounded by a bomb which exploded on his foot. Although in great pain, he gave directions for the counter-attack to be continued, and this was done successfully, about 100 prisoners and six machine-guns being taken. Without doubt the high courage and determination displayed by Lieut Col Hudson saved a serious situation, and had it not been for his quick determination in organizing a counter-attack a large number of the enemy would have dribbled through. A counter-attack on a larger scale would have been necessary to restore the situation.

Hudson did not rejoin the Battalion. He was evacuated to the UK, and underwent surgical treatment in London where he was frequently visited by Vera Brittain, seeking news of her brother's death. She obtained little information from Hudson, as he had left the ridge before the battle area was cleared, and the Battle Narrative written. The exact time, location and manner of Brittain's death remain undetermined.

Hudson recovered, served as Brigade Major in the North Russia force, then as a Staff Officer in what is now Malaya and became Chief Instructor at Sandhurst.

He then commanded a brigade at Aldershot, served in the BEF in the Second World War and was appointed CB for operations around Dunkirk. He commanded a division in the Home Forces until 1944 when he was appointed ADC to the King. General Hudson died in April 1959 in the Scilly Isles.

Other awards

The action at San Sisto Ridge earned the 11/Sherwood Foresters congratulations and medals. General Diaz mentioned the battalion in an official communiqué, and all ranks were publicly congratulated by the GOC 23rd Division for their behaviour in the battle.

Apart from Lieutenant Colonel Hudson's VC, he also received the Italian *Medaglia d'Argento Al Valor Militare* and the *Croix de Guerre.* There werre awards of a Bar to the DSO to Major Young, and a DSO to Captain Horsley. Captain Bird, and Second Lieutenants Sallmayer, Clifton and Cheetham were award the Military Cross. Sergeant Ellis received a Bar to his DCM, and CSM J Betts, Privates Springall and Groom were awarded the medal. Seventeen men received the MM or Bar including Sergeant RH Edwards, the Battalion Transport Sergeant. In addition, thirteen Foresters were 'Mentioned' in General Cavan's Despatch of 14 September 1918 for action during the battle. The men of B Company 8/KOYLI were not forgotten; awards included a Bar to the MC, four DCMs, six MMs or bars, and a Croix de Guerre while Captain Horsley was awarded the DSO. The help received from the Allies was recognized; *Commandant* Farques, 108ᵉ RI, was recommended for the DSO, and the names of three other French soldiers were submitted for awards, also that of *Maggiore* Van Den Heuval and three of his men.

On 12 July an Anglo-French parade was held at Granezza for the investiture of British and French honours. The troops were selected from those who had fought side by side on 15 June; and the parade included two companies of Sherwood Foresters, a detachment from the 8/KOYLI under Captain Horsley, and men from the 108ᵉ and 126ᵉ RI. The British received their national awards from Lord Cavan, and General Graziani presented the *Croix de Guerre avec Palme* to Major, now Lieutenant Colonel, Young, the *Croix de Guerre avec Etoile* (Bronze) to Captain Bird, CSM S Thompson (B Company) Lance Corporal G Main, while Lance Corporal F Stafford received the same award, but with a white metal star. General Babington received the *Croix de Geurre avec Palme.* Lord Cavan decorated Colonel Bontemps, 126ᵉ RI, with the DSO. *Commandant* Farques and Lieutenant Gautier received the MC, and five of their soldiers the MM. No record of the presence of Italian mortarmen at the ceremony, has been located, nor of any awards being awarded elsewhere.

The Foresters suffered relatively few casualties; 1 officer and 7 ORs killed, 3 officers and 41 ORs wounded, and 3 missing. Several more men died of their wounds in a Casualty Clearing Station at Dueville, on the plain below the plateau, their injuries aggravated by the terrible journey down the face of the escarpment by ambulance.

Edward Brittain's body was removed from the front line along with the rest of the dead of A Company, and laid to rest in a nearby British cemetery. Hugh Dalton wrote that:

> Not till the end of May did Spring really climb the mountains, and the snow finally vanish, and then the days, apart from the facts of war, were perfect, blue sky and sunshine all day long among the warm aromatic pines and the freshness of the mountain air. Here and there, in clearings in the forest, were patches of thick, rich grass, making a bright contrast to the dull, dark green of the pines, and in the grass arose many-coloured wild flowers. The Italians have buried their dead up here in little groups among the trees, and not in great graveyards. There was one such little group on the hillside in the middle of our Battery position, between two of our gun pits. There was another in the middle of our forward position at San Sisto, and another, where some thirty Bersaglieri and Artillerymen were buried, in the Barental Valley. It was here one day that an Irish Major, newly come to Italy, said to me, 'I don't want any better grave than that'. Nor did I. It was a place of marvellous and eternal beauty, ever changing with the seasons. It made one's heart ache to be in the midst of it. It was hither that they brought in the months that followed many of the British dead, who fell in this sector, and laid them beside the Italians, at whose graves we had looked.

After the Armistice the cemetery was relocated. Many of the bodies were re-interred at Granezza Cemetery, near the southern end of the valley, and in the lea of M. Corno. This is a very quiet and peaceful place, and no less beautiful than the silent woods of the Barental Valley.

Vera Brittain was haunted by her brother's death for the rest of her days. Her ashes were taken to Italy by her daughter, later Baroness Shirley Williams, and sprinkled on Edward's grave. The 11/Sherwood Foresters' War Diary makes no mention of the death of Brittain, nor indeed does it give casualty figures for the battle. *The Men from the Greenwood* mentions his death only as part of the casualty list of fifty-five dead, wounded and missing.

9/York and Lancasters

The 9/Y&L, to the left of the Sherwood Foresters, were also fiercely attacked. The battalion had two platoon picquets out, watching for any movement around Ave and Poslen. When enemy troops were seen coming through the wire word was sent back to the front line. Both platoons engaged the first wave of enemy. One picquet withdrew safely but the other, consisting of Lieutenant Kempton and twenty men, hung on too long and after a bitter battle were overwhelmed. Only two men escaped to tell the tale.

The battalion position was attacked by large numbers of the enemy who flooded over the low ridge, bringing machine-guns and large quantities of ammunition and supported by heavy artillery and mortar fire. Throughout the day it conducted a straightforward defensive battle. The *k.u.k.* assault units made three frontal attacks but each was defeated by rifle and machine-gun fire.

Clearing the battlefield

Early the next morning 16th June the battalion sent a reconnaissance patrol to Ave Ridge, and Poslen. After checking Guardinalti, the patrol continued over the ridge and in the shallow valley beyond, found two abandoned artillery pieces and dragged them back to the British front line. Later, other patrols brought in machine-guns, *Flammenwerfer,* and a case of gas shells, although it is not recorded whether these were for the mountain guns. No Man's Land was described by all patrols as being covered with the bodies of dead and wounded soldiers.

Night watch

The night of 16/17 June was disturbed by enemy patrols which crept up to the British wire and fired rifle-grenades and flares into the trenches. Cheering was heard from No Man's Land, and the 13/DLI, on the left of the 9/Y&L, called down an SOS barrage on the line of the Poslen-Guardinalti ridge. Shortly afterwards the Austrian patrols fired a great number of flares which revealed large numbers of the enemy retreating across the shallow valley of the Ghelpac, between Morar and Ave. And that ended the battle, as far as the 9/Y&L was concerned.

68 Brigade - Monte Kaberlaba

Monte Kaberlaba dominated the centre of the British sector. 68 Brigade had three battalions in the front line, right, 13/Durham Light Infantry; 12/DLI centre and, left, 11/Northumberland Fusiliers with 10/Northumberland Fusiliers (support) on M. Torle, holding about 2,500 metres of front. The brigade was attacked at around 7.30 am. The two Durham battalions were little troubled but the 11/Northumberland Fusiliers on the left of the line, in Grimsby Trench, had a lively time, and a few Austrians briefly entered, but did not breach, the front line. Norman Gladden wrote a vivid description of some of the fighting:

We had a good position for the gun but no shelter from the elements. Fortunately the night was clear and bright, though cold. Our guns strafed occasionally, but between their half-hearted outbursts everywhere seemed very still. We had a patrol out and were instructed to keep a keen watch for them. Thus, in the early hours of 15th June 1918, muffled in my great-coat, I huddled into a corner of the fire-step. I was too cold to do more than doze or twist restlessly in a half-dream. I heard the scrunch of passing feet and a voice talking to the sentries. It sounded miles away, weary and worried. It was Captain Stirling's voice, saying that a gas attack was expected and that we were to keep a sharp look out. This instruction was to be passed on to other sentries. I smiled. This was the sort of nonsense one heard in dreams. A gas attack up here? The Austrians had no guns; they rarely bothered to reply to any provocation. I dozed off again and then woke with a jolt. It was my turn for sentry. I slipped drowsily into the trench. I had not dreamed the captain's words after all: they were repeated now. The wind was right up about something. During our turn we discussed the problem endlessly but could get no reason out of it. Out in front all was quiet, except for an occasional Very light, and we had nothing further to report to our relief.

Orders to stand to had been passed along just before daybreak. Crouching forms were stirring and straightening up on all sides, when something began to happen. Guns were firing out in front, actually out in front! Flashes lit up the hills on the far side of the plateau and a roar of artillery rolled along the entire front. A crescendo of sound and then the storm burst upon us. Screaming shells rushed to earth amidst the wire, and behind us, or further over in the woods. Lumps of rock were hurled about by the explosions. The trench soon became swathed in a cloud of acrid smoke. My first impulse was to laugh. No guns! Good God! Here was a real slap-up barrage on the Western Front pattern. And soon our own artillery would join in.

Some of the patrol appeared through the haze; there had already been casualties and the officer [2nd Lt Youll - see below] was missing. Coloured lights went up out of the valley. The

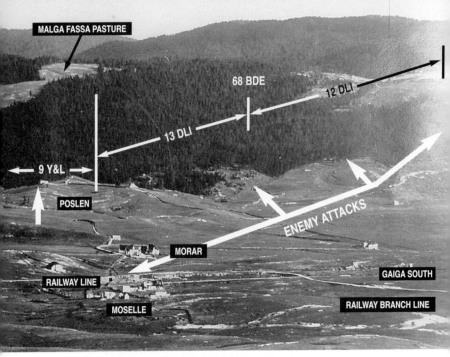

Labels on image: MALGA FASSA PASTURE, 68 BDE, 12 DLI, 13 DLI, 9 Y&L, POSLEN, ENEMY ATTACKS, MORAR, RAILWAY LINE, MOSELLE, GAIGA SOUTH, RAILWAY BRANCH LINE

9 York & Lancaster's and 68 Brigade, sectors.

enemy's barrage continued unabated, but our own guns remained silent. Corporal Goffee decided to work up the trench to the right into a quieter and more commanding position. We dodged from bay to bay, now pushing past crouching figures and

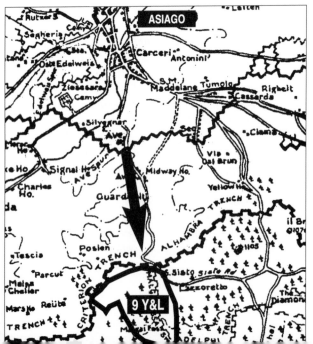

Labels on map: ASIAGO, 9 Y&L

June 1918, area held by 9/York & Lancasters and probable Austrian threat axis.

exchanging an oath here and there, now crouching ourselves as a shell burst nearer than usual. We reached a suitable spot and then discovered that we had left behind some of the spares and magazines. I went back with the corporal. The shells were dropping with awful regularity about the trench; only the hardness of the ground saved us from being buried. But this protective hardness had a terror of its own, as lumps of rock and stone hailed down into the trench. A few tremulous seconds and we had retrieved our stuff and were on the way back, ducking and hesitating at each bend. A particularly fearful blast kept me rooted in a more sheltered corner. A man beside me crouched against the parapet hugging his rifle. In the sickly glare I recognised Bully Peterson. 'This is hell', he muttered, gritting his teeth, 'as bad as Ypres. The bleeding fools to bring us into this without warning.' Although this was a man whom I disliked intensely I could not find a good reason to disagree with him on this occasion.

Over my shoulder, as I crouched, I could see the bursts of incendiary shells, and, as I watched, a tremendous flame rose up as some of the trees caught fire. The flames leapt up like gigantic red seas beating against a breakwater and flowed through the gaunt trees which banked up the hillside above us. It was a terrifying but magnificent sight. I rejoined the section breathless but unhurt. The bombardment continued. Heavy shells streamed over like express trains, to burst in the further recesses of the hills, with a shattering roar which could be heard even above the general bombardment. Cries for stretcher-bearers began to arise on our left, and from time to time word was passed along that some poor devil was wounded or 'had got the knock'. Who would be next?

There were some dug-outs in the trench, deep shafts with openings facing the enemy lines. Why the Italians had constructed them thus, I could not understand. There was one in the very bay we were now occupying. The shells were falling so close to the trench that any cover seemed better than the open trench. Consequently the dug-out began to fill. I found a place in the entrance and was soon lulled into a sense of false security. The flying rock could not hit one there. An officer came dodging along the trench; when he discovered the crowded dug-out he was rightly indignant. He threatened, cajoled and almost cried, but this was no time for him to wield his authority effectively. For

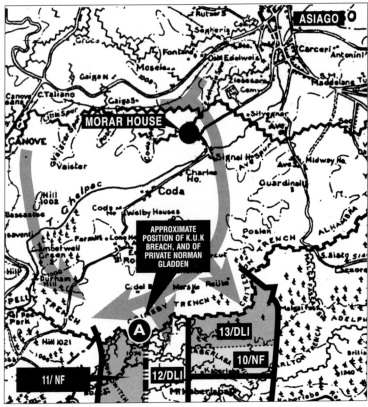

Layout of 68 Brigade 14-16 June 1918.

my part, I knew he was right, but it felt so secure under the sheltering rock - and there were NCOs among us. We knew that only a direct hit was likely to finish us off there, whereas out in the trench anything might happen.

As it was I spent my time half in and half out of the shelter, according to the intensity of shelling. After a time one gets used to this sort of thing. Reports came up from the valley that were anything but reassuring, and there could be little doubt that our losses were severe and increasing. All the time there was the question in my mind: what was the shelling about? Was this the enemy's accumulated revenge for many pinpricks? It is strange that the truth did not dawn upon us, for none of us took the business really seriously.

A cry of 'Gas!' jerked me out of my musings, and the acrid fumes of a shell-burst close by caused me to imagine that the gas

78

was already upon us. I adjusted my box respirator excitedly, taking more time than was usual on parade and, my companions having done likewise, we crouched round in our weird garb puffing through our rubber mouthpieces and looking like other-world creatures from a novel by H.G. Wells. One man made a sorry mess of adjusting his helmet, got a whiff of gas and had to be taken to higher ground further up the trench to await his chance of getting out. The bombardment, owing no doubt to the use of gas shells, appeared at this juncture to become less severe.

No news had come up from the valley since the alarm had sounded and two of us went along to regain contact. The next bay was badly shattered and seemed to be full of gas. We encountered the sergeant-major a little lower down, who signalled that all was OK and waved us back to our position.

The shelling continued, but a little later the 'all clear' having been passed along for gas, we took off our respirators and found the atmosphere bearable. However, the stench of high explosives was so overwhelming that it is doubtful whether we should have detected the presence of gas. We could tell through the smoke that the sun was now up; the bombardment seemed to have been going on for hours.

Our trench was manned. The barrage had receded into the woods behind us. A crackle of rifle fire came from among the trees on our left front; a red light shot up in the valley. And still our artillery maintained their extraordinary silence. The rifle fire developed into an unbroken rattle and it was obvious that the enemy were working their way through the woods towards the front line. Rifle shots and occasional Lewis gun bursts were directed from our trench but we were at a disadvantage, despite our fine view along the flank. In front the ground sloped away some fifty yards or so on this side of the wire, and movements further down the gully were hidden from us. The edge of the woods, where the enemy was still massing, was too far away for effective fire. After one or two experimental bursts with the gun, Corporal Goffee decided to conserve ammunition. I borrowed a rifle and took one or two long shots. Thus, nearly two years after I first went to France, I had my first shot at the enemy. On the Western Front, even in an offensive, one rarely saw him until he was a prisoner.

The thrill of fear experienced at the announcement of the attack had soon subsided and now, standing in the shelter of our

79

rock-hewn trench with a part of the battlefield stretched before me, I felt a curiosity that mastered all other feelings. I was now witnessing a battle from a viewpoint that a press correspondent might have envied. The occasional shell-burst behind our parados had little significance after the recent ordeal, and at this stage our job of holding the trench did not seem likely to be a difficult one.

And

At this moment the battle seemed to come to a stop. Then, with a thunderous report, the wood literally burst into flames and a tremendous cloud of muck and fumes shot into the air. The dump from which we had drawn our stores had blow up. At the time this was so closely synchronized with the flow of battle that we concluded that our withdrawing troops had fired the dump and that the enemy had suffered a momentary check. If so, this certainly did not last long. Enemy troops penetrated further to the rear and bullets began to flick over the back of our trench. [The battalion formed a defensive flank on their left, reinforced by some Vickers guns from 23rd Bn MGC and one company of the 10/Northumberland Fusiliers.] *We had the unwelcome feeling of being surrounded, though of course this was an exaggeration. I thought of the small forces behind us, of the close proximity of the plains, and the possibility of disaster loomed in my mind. Coloured lights now went up from behind, signals no doubt to the enemy artillery for them to move their barrage further over while, out in front, groups of the enemy continued to manoeuvre unmolested except by distant and therefore very chancy rifle fire.*

Crack! Crack! Shots came from the rear across the back of the trench as the enemy enfiladed us. The third act of the show was about to unfold itself. Enemy troops were spotted in the gully below us and the whole trench opened out with a roar. But the bulging ground sheltered the attackers until they got close to the wires. Then we were astounded to see a small party appear right up at the wire in the dip straight in front of the company. They were apparently in dead ground as far as our left flank was concerned, for no fire was directed against them from the lower end of the trench. The attackers, appearing to enjoy charmed lives, then put something into the wire and ran back quickly. The bomb or torpedo exploded with considerable concussion, blowing a complete section of the wire into the air and clearing a passage through the belt. It was an amazing feat. A party of the enemy then rushed the gap under cover of the dense smoke from the explosion, and were in the trench in a matter of seconds.

Almost simultaneously a stooping figure appeared above the brow about twenty-five yards in front of us, an enemy soldier bowed down with the weight of some infernal contrivance, a flame-thrower as we subsequently discovered. The trench belched fire from end to end and the poor brave devil fell forward on the skyline riddled by dozens of bullets. With one's knowledge of the possibilities of this fiery weapon, who can say how near to success this lone attacker had come? His companions, if he had any, failed to come into view, though we continued to keep a wary eye in that direction.

Our position was getting precarious. From below came the noise of bursting bombs and rifle shots fired between the close sides of the trench. All we could see were the black shapes of the missiles as they were lobbed from one bay to the next. The enemy were establishing themselves. We aligned our gun along the trench, but there was little we could do without the risk of hitting our own people. Bullets kept hitting the parapet, causing us to bob up and down like marionettes. The remnants of the company began to flow up the trench past us and we had visions of a general withdrawal over the hill to our right. A member of the left platoon came up, blackened from head to foot by a close-bursting bomb and almost demented with the concussion. He named pals trapped and wounded, before he collapsed on the firestep and the stretcher-bearers took a hand. Others came by, half-shell-shocked and demoralized. The enemy were gaining ground. Corporal Harkins came into the bay, looking for spare ammunition. He sent a man up the trench over the brow to beg, borrow or steal supplies from our neighbours. The NCOs were at their wits' end. Our gun was useless in this sort of engagement.

Then the miracle happened. At this critical moment leadership began to operate. Captain Stirling, looking taller and more gaunt than ever, appeared on the parados and called for volunteers to counter-attack the captured section. Electrified by his example and glad at seeing a possible solution to a grisly dilemma, the men in our part of the trench, raising a shout, began to clamber up after him. We were all carried away by a real wave of enthusiasm, and the section would have abandoned the gun to a man if level-headed Corporal Goffee had not ordered us back to our position to support the forward *movement. The attacking party was quickly marshalled into line by the captain and the sergeant-major, who had also come on to the scene. These two tall figures, waving the line forward, set off in the forefront of the attack, which was in effect a move to storm our own positions. It was a magnificent movement and a glorious sight. The two leaders, slightly ahead, striding forward and swinging like catapults as they hurled their Mills bombs, followed by the improvised line of riflemen with bayonets fixed, pivoted from the back of the trench and converged in a half circle upon the unobstructed rear of the captured section. Their bombs were soon bursting about the position. Our invaders did not await the impact. Feeling, no doubt, that too much could be asked of mere flesh and blood, they left the trench in disorder and fled towards the woods, while our men disappeared into the trench with a cheer, which was taken up by all of us. Hitherto I had seen no one fall and our casualties must have so far been very light. But now tragedy intervened. Elated by their success, the excited attackers leapt up on to the parapet with the obvious intention of following the retreating enemy. This was a foolish and unnecessary thing to do, only to be accounted for by the uncontrolled excitement of the moment. Already the Austrians had got far and the baffled pursuers began to snipe at them with their rifles. Enemy troops occupying the surrounding woods immediately opened fire, and many of our company fell never to rise again. A few survivors scattered back into the trench as best they could.*

The company's position was again intact. From our vantage point we had been little more than spectators of this action, since our men were between us and the enemy most of the time. Fire from our end of the trench ahead had therefore been desultory. But it was all over in a matter of seconds.

During the battle the battalion was reinforced by two companies of the 10/Northumberland Fusiliers who were in support at M. Torle, to the south of M. Kaberlaba. One company strengthened the defensive flank, as noted above, the other remained in support on the southern slopes of M. Kaberlaba.

At 9 pm the 10/Northumberland Fusiliers relieved the 11th, who were reinforced by two companies and the battalion headquarters of 8/Y&L. The fusilier company in the defensive flank was withdrawn into the support lines on M. Kaberlaba. The 10/NF Fusiliers suffered two dead and twenty-three injured in the course of the battle, and 11/NF 109 casualties, including twenty-nine dead.

Aftermath

Norman Gladden also wrote that :

There was an interesting event on 30 July when the battalion paraded with great ceremony to witness the presentation of the VC to 2nd/Lt Youll of C Company...

This was the second VC to be awarded for bravery during the Battle of Asiago.

Youll, Second-Lieutenant John Scott, 11th Battalion The Northumberland Fusiliers Victoria Cross – London Gazette – 11.7.1918: For most conspicuous bravery and devotion to duty during enemy attacks when in command of a patrol, which came under the hostile barrage. Sending his men back to safety, he remained to observe the situation. Unable to subsequently rejoin his company, 2nd Lieutenant Youll reported to a neighbouring unit, and when the enemy attacked he maintained his position with several men of different units until the troops on his left had given way and an enemy machine-gun opened fire from behind him. He rushed the gun and, having killed most of the team, opened fire on the enemy with the captured gun, inflicting heavy casualties. Then, finding that the enemy had gained a footing in a portion of the front line, he organized and carried out with a few men three separate counter-attacks. On each occasion he drove back the enemy, but was unable to maintain his position by reason of reverse fire. Throughout the fighting his complete disregard of personal safety and very gallant leading set a magnificent example to all.

Youll was also awarded the Italian Silver Medal for Valour. He was killed in action on the River Piave during the Battle of Vittorio Veneto, on 27th October 1918, aged twenty-one. He is buried in Giavera Cemetery, on the side of the Montello, within sight of the river, and of the Asiago plateau.

Chapter Six

CARRIOLA
The Battle in the Woods

The 48th (South Midlands) Division occupied the left (Carriola) sector, defending a front of about 4,500 metres although the actual length of the trench line was nearer 6,000 mertres. The front line of necessity mainly meandered through thick woodland, following (roughly) the 1,000 metre contour. The division had two brigades forward: 143 (Lt. Col. LLC Reynolds, 1/1 Bucks, in temporary command) (left, Cesuna Switch, with one battalion in the line) and 145 (Brig. GC Sladen) (right, Ghelpac Fork, two battalion's in the line), with 144 (Lt. Col. FM Tomkinson, 1/7 Worcs, in temporary command) Brigade in reserve at Carriola. All units were under-strength through the ravages of flu, the need to provide troops (mainly from the infantry battalions) to man the long supply lines down the escarpment, and the usual rotation of men to training schools, or for a precious week's rest at the newly-opened leave centre in Sirmione on Lake Garda. In addition, two of the three brigade commanders were away, and six of the battalions were commanded by majors, the COs being either sick, on leave or acting as temporary brigade commanders. During the battle the division was attacked by elements of two *k.u.k.* divisions (6th and 52nd). The attackers came from the 6th, 17th, 27th, 74th *Freiherr von Schonaich,* 81st and 127th infantry regiments, about seventeen battalions in all. The front line was quickly breached in four places,

Carriola base, June 1999. Looking south west to M. Pau. FRANCIS MACKAY.

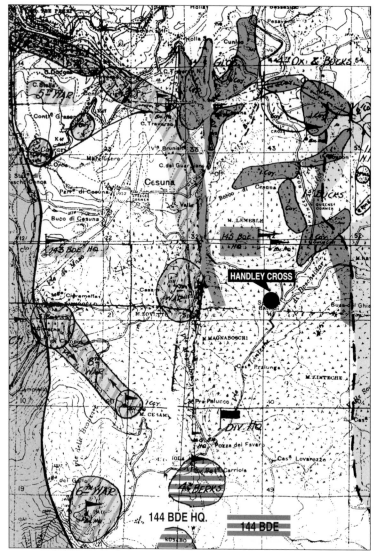

Layout of 48th Division, 15-16 June 1918.

and the defenders required twenty-four hours of hard fighting before the attackers were evicted.

General Fanshawe

The division was commanded by Major-General Sir Robert Fanshawe KCB DSO, the 'Chocolate Soldier', one of three brothers, all generals and, in 1918, all on active service. He had been commissioned into the Ox & Bucks LI in 1883, seen active service on the North West Frontier and in South Africa, where he served for nearly three years. He had a diffident air and was reckoned to be mildly eccentric. His nickname derived from the habit of carrying a satchel of chocolate bars which he distributed to soldiers he met along the way. He was invariably pleasant to junior officers, and polite to everyone he met. The officers of the 1/7 Worcesters remembered with affection his sending champagne up to their Mess after an arduous time in the trenches. Many staff officers disliked him, probably because of his 'bag of chocolate', but as a commander he was respected by the soldiery, who are stern but usually accurate judges of those set over them.

Layout

In accordance with the Corps Defence Scheme a picquet line had been established about five hundred yards ahead of the front line trenches. In this sector the line consisted of lightly wired positions on low hills, garrisoned at night by a platoon (with outposts close to the enemy wire, and backed up by roving patrols) and by day, a section.

48th Division front: opposing front lines, and British forward positions.

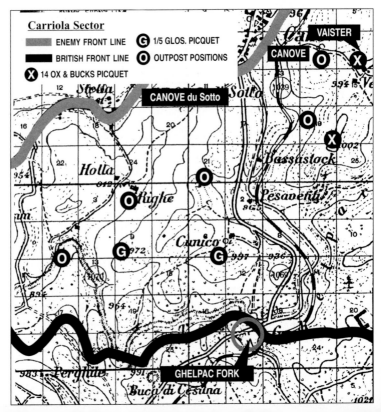

The outposts and picquets were little troubled by the enemy, despite being, in some cases, very close to his trenches.

Attack routes

In this sector a pair of natural attack routes ran from the Austrian lines at Canove deep into the British rear area. These attack routes ran through small valleys running north and south to the Ghelpac valley. Both offered easy access by infantry and light artillery to within yards of the British wire, and beyond that to Cesuna, Carriola and Campiello, and were familiar to the Austrians, from the *Strafexpedition*, and they intended using both routes in *Radetzky*. The British also recognized the value of these routes, and intended using them during and after their June offensive and had cleared them of obstacles and built tracks, some stretches of which were metalled. The *k.u.k.* kept an interested (and grateful) eye on progress, but did not interfere. Captain VF Eberle, a Territorial RE officer who served throughout the war in 48th Division, wrote of conducting a survey in No Man's Land shortly before the *k.u.k.* attack. He spotted an Austrian officer and a companion on a similar errand a couple of hundred yards away. The Austrian raised his

48th Division front: *k.u.k.* attack routes.

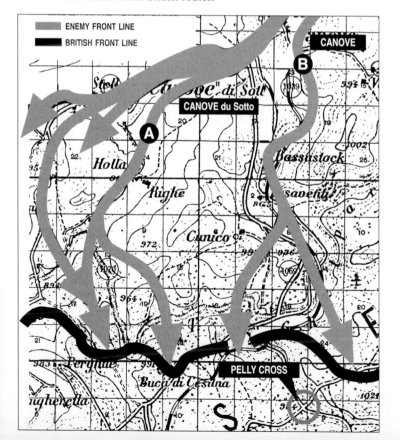

Carriola sector: part of the attack route from Canove di Sotto to Happy Valley and the Valle Gap (A) on map page 87. FRANCIS MACKAY

arm in greeting, then both parties went about their business. Eberle did not attach any significance to this chance encounter despite warnings of a possible Austrian offensive.

The first route ran from near Canove station into the British front line at Ghelpac Fork, then southwards into the forest. The second ran from Canove di Sotto (Lower Canove) to the Ghelpac: its lower reaches were referred to as 'Holla Valley' by the British. It reached the Ghelpac opposite Happy Valley which lead to the hamlet of Valle, east of the village of Cesuna. This was the most important point of the divisional sector, and, unfortunately, the weakest.

Valle 'Gap'

This was the key to the western sector of the Allied defences on the plateau. Here, where the Cesuna Switch met Polygon Trench and Lemerle Switch, ran D Track, connecting Carriola to No Man's Land via D Gap, a lane in the front line wire. Just outside the wire Z Track led eastwards to a temporary gun position near some ruins below Hill 972. The British had used these tracks to dump defence stores in No Man's Land, some as far as a thousand yards forward of the front line. The wire in the Valle Gap had several lanes cut through it, both official and unofficial. These had been made in preparation for the Allied offensive and to allow vehicles to reach the front line and No Man's Land. The Italians also used these gaps as a short-cut to avoid

Carriola sector: upper reaches of the attack route from Canove station to Ghelpac Fork (B) on map page 87. FRANCIS MACKAY

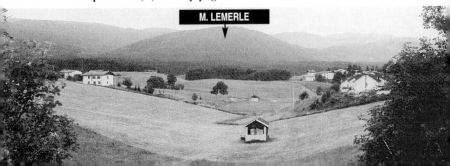

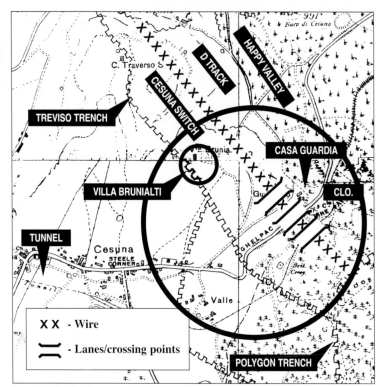

The 'Valle Gap'.

congestion at Handley Cross, when travelling between X Corps to their countrymen in the defences east of the French, by way of Pine Avenue and Pria dell' Acqua. (Mainly at night or in mist or rain, as the road through Cesuna was in full view of *k.u.k* OPs.)

After Valle the attack route wound round the base of M. Lemerle, and up into a combe, the Val Magnaboschi, vital to both sides. It contained a key Allied cross-roads (Bosky Junction), and it would have lead the Austrians either south to Carriola, west over Zovetto Ridge to Campiello, or northwest to outflank the Italian defences on the western end of the plateau. So Valle was where the *k.u.k* would have to go, and where they had to be held. It was the key point in the defences, but not only was it inadequately fortified, it was also the junction of two incomplete switches, and on an inter-brigade boundary, and its importance appears to have been overlooked in the defence plan.

Defences

The British front line trenches were protected by a belt of wire which in some places extended down and into the river bed, which was only full of water in the spring thaw. At many points in the front line

Cross section, trenches along south bank of Ghelpac River, 48th Div front.

the pitch of the slope was so acute that soldiers had to lean over the parapet to fire at attackers. The thick woodland restricted vision and arcs of fire, and allowed enemy patrols to approach the wire unseen. They did so, and as part of the preparations for *Radetzky* Austrian patrols examined the Allied front line in detail, noting patrol lanes, and estimating the strength and disposition of the defence. They would have noticed the sparsity of troops in the line, and might have overheard musters when the number of men reporting, or reported, sick could be heard. Austrian scouts may also have penetrated the British rear areas to note the precise location of dumps and headquarters: the Italians certainly knew that 'close target reconnaissance' took place and practised a form of it themselves, using teams drawn from the ranks of the *Guardia di Finanza* (Customs Guards, then as now a military body in Italy) and some of their erstwhile smuggler opponents.

Forward areas

The *k.u.k.* had been over the ground occupied by the British, during the 1916 *Strafexpedition,* and Cesuna village was one of the places they had seen before. It had long been evacuated, but contained some road junctions and a railway tunnel, used by the British to house defence stores and as an excellent shelter when the *k.u.k.* mounted a strafe. Before the war Cesuna had been home to a small community of wood-cutters, dairy farmers, and some railwaymen. One family had lived in a track-side house beyond Valle. This appears on maps and in accounts of the battle as 'Clo', or C[lo] , a corruption of *Casello*, a dwelling built by railway companies for permanent-way gangers and their families. [See map page 89.]

M. Lemerle

Behind the British front line lay several support lines. Lemerle

Switch lay along the lower north face of that hill. In spring 1918 the switch was little more than a line of wire entanglements and a trench; it lacked traverses, strong-points and shell-proof dug-outs. M. Lemerle had seen savage fighting during the *Strafexpedition* when it was stormed by the Austrians during their final lunge at the escarpment. The Italians beat them off, but it was a close-fought battle. In June 1918 various headquarters were situated on the southern slope, connected to Carriola by a communication trench which is not only still visible but walkable. On the western flank of M. Lemerle defence galleries were built into the slopes of the hill, part of Polygon Trench, a leg of Lemerle Switch. [See map page 84]. On the east side of M. Lemerle lay Orchard Trench, and above that Oxford Trench, both of which met near Swiss Cottage, a Field Ambulance site on Princes Road. Poelderhook Trench, another leg of Lemerle Switch, also ended at this point, the trench line continuing across (under) Princes road to become Jargon Trench.

Cesuna Switch

Lemerle Switch was linked to the front line by the Cesuna Switch which consisted of Treviso Trench and some wire entanglements. The switch passed Villa Brunialti, once a holiday home but in June 1918 a battered shell, then dipped into a re-entrant below Casa Traverso South to meet the Asiago road and the front line above the Ghelpac Gorge. From that point a communication trench ran back over Perghele Ridge to re-join the front line above the mouth of Happy Valley.

M. Lemerle: Italian war memorials.
FRANCIS MACKAY

Cross routes

East of Bosky Junction a rough track, Lemerle Road, wound over a col between M. Lemerle and M. Magnaboschi, then down to Handley Cross where it met Princes Road. South of Handley Cross this became Cavan Road. Beyond Handley Cross 'Lemerle' became 'Langabissa' Road which lead to Pria dell'Acqua. This lateral route was especially popular with Italian staff officers and couriers travelling between the First and Sixth Armies, and with British traffic between the front line,

Carriola and Pria dell'Acqua. Handley Cross was always busy, as it was not only a key crossroads but the site of a telephone circuit junction, and of several supply and material dumps. In June 1918, as mentioned earlier, these included a huge dump of artillery and trench mortar ammunition, stacked close to the crossroads ready for the intended Allied offensive.

Marginal line

At the head of the Val Magnaboschi, along an outlying ridge of M. Ceramella, lay yet another row of trenches, a part of the Marginal Line. Behind this lay the Carriola base, housing the divisional headquarters and that of the rear brigade and the divisional machine-gun battalion. There was also sufficient accommodation for three infantry battalions and various support units. The base sprawled over several wide basins at the top of the escarpment, connected to the plains by Connaught Road, and *mulaterria* leading down to Chiuppano and Caltrano. The Marginal Road ran along the escarpment to Tattenham Corner, and was lined with dumps, reservoirs and pumping stations, and *teleferiche* stations for lines coming from the plains or running up into the hills.

Dispositions

On the right 145 Brigade [see map page 85] defended a front of about 1500 metres, nearly all in the woods to the south of Ghelpac Fork ('Ghelpac Park' in some sources). The 1/4 Ox & Bucks LI (Lieutenant-Colonel AJN Bartlett) had two companies in the front line (Pelly Trench), and two in depth near battalion headquarters, in a sunken lane off Prince's Road. The 1/5 Gloucesters (Major NH Waller) held

Villa Brunialti after the fighting.

forward left, in very broken ground and woods. In support were 1/1 Bucks Bn (Major PA Hall) manning Poelderhook Trench and part of Lemerle Switch. 1/4 Royal Berks (Lieutenant-Colonel AB Lloyd Baker) were in reserve near Carriola. The Ox & Bucks manned picquets on Hill 1002 and at a ruined farm on the tip of Vaister Spur, and 1/5 Gloucesters manned those on Cunico Hill and Hill 972. Brigade Headquarters was located on the southern slopes of M. Lemerle, near the OP tunnel.

On the left 143 Brigade, holding some 3,000 yards of front, was dispersed, apparently at random, between the Ghelpac Gorge and Carriola. Brigade Headquarters were on Hill 1152 to the south west of Cesuna. The front line (Thinle Trench) was held by 1/5 Warwicks (Lieutenant-Colonel EAM Bindloss), with two companies in the trenches and two in depth. 1/7 Warwicks (Lieutenant-Colonel JM Knox) were Divisional Reserve, in the Val Magnaboschi; while 1/8 Warwicks (Major PH Whitehouse) had one company in the Cesuna Switch; two more in Busibollo Camp, a cluster of huts on a hillside overlooking Campiello, and battalion headquarters and the remaining company in trenches on M. Ceramella. 1/6 Warwicks (Lieutenant-Colonel WM Pryor)were in reserve at Carriola. This layout provided considerable flexibility in countering an enemy breakthrough. The front line was lightly manned, with only two weak companies covering well over 2,000 metres of trenches, but a quick look at the map on page 85 reveals that the rest of the brigade was well-placed to intervene right and left of Zovetto Ridge.

144 Brigade was in reserve. Brigade Headquarters was at M Carriola, 1/4 Gloucesters (Major E Shellard) and 1/7 Worcesters (Major JP Bate) were in foothill villages, 1/6 Gloucesters (Lieutenant-Colonel HSG Schomberg) were at Serona Camp, east of Carriola, and 1/8 Worcesters (Lieutenant-Colonel HT Clarke) at M. Brusabo Camp, perched on the edge of the world by the escarpment rim.

Preparations

During the morning of 14th June Fanshawe attended a conference at Corps HQ where up-to-date information about the imminent enemy attack was divulged to the divisional commanders. During the afternoon, at very short notice, the general summoned brigade and unit commanders to a conference at Carriola. There he announced that the Allied offensive on the enemy front line, set for 18th June, had been postponed as there was reliable evidence that the rumoured, and long-delayed, Austrian offensive would be mounted next day along the

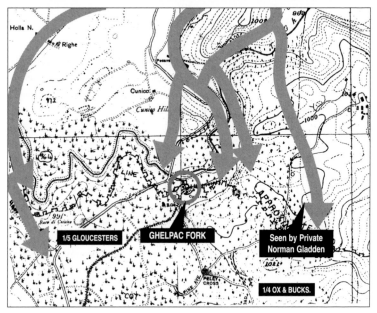

145 Brigade: company positions, and enemy attacks, 7.15am 15 June 1918.

entire Allied front, from the Adriatic to the River Adige. He said that the latest Italian intelligence assessment was that on the plateau the main *k.u.k.* attack would probably be directed at the Italian defences at the eastern end of it and the French positions in the centre, and that while the British would probably be bombarded with HE and gas, they might not be attacked. He stated they should prepare for the worst and reiterated the main precautions required for an active defence, including counter-attack plans and artillery fire-plans. Few officers appear to have believed an attack would take place after so many false alarms, but nevertheless they set about preparing for defence rather than attack. The outpost line, fortunately, was well-manned, to protect preparations for the now abandoned Allied offensive.

Opening rounds.

According to *The Worcestershire Regiment in the Great War:*

The Austrian artillery opened an intense bombardment, plastering with shells every British battery position and every cross roads. The great dump of shells at Handley Cross was hit. There was a terrific explosion, followed by continuous minor explosions as outlying portions of the great dump blew up in their turn. The dump was situated at the principal cross roads in the area and the explosions, which continued for several hours, paralyzed all movement or communication from front to rear. The bombardment began at 3 a.m. The Austrian gunnery was very

94

good and their information was obviously accurate and complete. Every Battalion Headquarters and Company Headquarters of the battalions holding the line was hit and all telephone wires were cut. The latter were not buried owing to the rocky nature of the soil.

During the night of 14 June a patrol from the Ox & Bucks picquet at Vaister attacked a small enemy post near Canove manned by the 23 *Honved* Infantrie Regiment and captured one prisoner, who was hustled back to Battalion Headquarters, located in a sunken lane off Prince's Road. The prisoner did not understand English or German, but indicated by signs that there was to be a heavy bombardment, including gas shells, just before 3 am, then an attack. The Battalion staff were sceptical of this information, despite the afternoon briefing, and at around 2 am sent the prisoner back to the Divisional Intelligence section. Lieutenant-Colonel GH Barnett, the Divisional AA & QMG, in *With the 48th Division in Italy*, recounts being wakened at around 3 am by someone looking for the Divisional Intelligence Officer, and that as he was drifting off to sleep again he heard strange sounds not unlike surf on a rocky shore. This was the enemy bombardment, right on time, and it created havoc with the forward defences, and made life very difficult for the brigade and divisional staff, whose Headquarters were subjected to a heavy barrage. The weather, as mentioned earlier,

145 Brigade *k.u.k.* approach routes and concentration areas, Val d' Assa, North of Canove Ridge.

was misty and damp, and what little visibility there might have been was lost through the large quantities of smoke, gas and dust thrown up by the barrage. The numerous divisional and brigade OPs could see nothing, but heard the sounds of rifle and machine-gun fire.

145 Brigade - Ghelpac Fork

The fighting in this area was particularly confused due to the dense woodland. The maps on page 103 give general outlines of the positions at the beginning, and height, of the Austrian penetration. Late on 14 June large numbers of enemy infantry had moved into assembly areas in caves and gullies in the deep gorge of the Val d'Assa below Canove Ridge. When the barrage started the troops had moved over the ridge by communication trenches and spread out along the front line. Large numbers went through lanes in the wire either side of Canove station into the attack route mentioned earlier. Here they quickly shook-out into assault formations and advanced down the gully, round or over the low hills into the woods in front of the Ox & Bucks defences. Part of their attack was seen by Norman Gladden:

Through the din, which had certainly lessened, we heard whistle blasts and were puzzled. Suddenly there was a shout from a watcher on the firestep to our right. 'Stand to! He is coming over!' A chill trickled down my spine. My first impulse was to deny the possibility. The enemy to come all that way across the plateau to attack us: that was an absurd idea! We grasped our weapons and rushed pell-mell to the firestep. The barrage was lifting. In front, beyond the belt of wire, a wall of white smoke drifted slowly away. Over to the left, where the tongue of forest stretched forward along the far side of the depression, through the dividing mists, I saw a remarkable sight. An officer in strange uniform on horseback was galloping up and down, marshalling a column of enemy troops into the woods, where they were quickly lost to view.

Part of the *k.u.k.* assault may have been marshalled by an officer on a white horse, but it was lead by *Sturmtruppen* armed like their colleagues at San Sisto with Bangalore torpedoes, shears, bombs, machine guns and *Flammenwerfer*. Gladden goes on:

Meanwhile things were getting lively in the woods. More coloured lights went up - despairingly it seemed - and the hollow crash of bombs punctuated the rattle of musketry. A stiff fight was being put up by our advance posts. Then I saw khaki figures running back, followed closely by grey lines of the enemy, moving more methodically, while reinforcements continued to stream across the plateau into the end of the wood now in the enemy's rear. The combatants drew parallel with us and well within rifle-shot, but we were unable to shoot as it was difficult to distinguish friend from foe in the melee. Our only task for the time being was to keep a look out over the slope in front. It was then, I think, that we began to realize that things were not going very favourably and that our own position was being threatened. We had no artillery support; the woods in front were crammed with Austrians. If only we could have dropped a barrage there at this juncture. But we did not. The troops in the wood below came to grips in earnest, but all details were blocked out by the clouds of smoke that curled among the trees. I saw the flash of cold steel and the stabbing flames from rifles fired at close quarters. The wood was being fiercely contested by the men of the 48th Division, but the enemy's onslaught was too heavy and the defenders continued to fall back, leaving our flank in the air.

In fact a breach had been made in the front line between 1/4 Ox & Bucks and 11/Northumberland Fusiliers, where Grimsby Trench was very light manned. Both battalions immediately formed defensive flanks, but the gap was not closed until later in the battle. The 23rd Bn Machine Gun Corps helped cover the breach, as described in their Battle Narrative:

At 8.45 a.m. Lieutenant LN VIZARD, who was in charge of guns in position at L.9 and L.10, having ascertained from the Machine Gun Guard on the Machine Gun Dump that the enemy had penetrated our front line on the right of the left division, and that the 11th Battalion Northumberland Fusiliers were forming a defensive flank, moved L.9 and L.10 guns to alternative positions so as to conform with this movement and protect the left flank. At 9 a.m. Captain JWH TOYNBEE MC received a message from this officer to this effect and immediately proceeded to this position, and on finding that the situation had been temporarily restored by a counter attack delivered by the right Battalion of the 48th Division, proceeded to H.Q., 11th Battalion Northumberland Fusiliers, to ascertain the exact situation. At about 10.15 a.m. the enemy again attacked and succeeded in establishing himself in the front line of the Right Company of the 48th Division. On being informed by the Adjutant 11th Battalion Northumberland Fusiliers that this Battalion was in need of bombs, Captain TOYNBEE sent a runner to his Company H.Q. with orders to form the personnel there into a carrying party to bring the bombs stored there to this Battalion. This party arrived shortly afterward and remained in position on the defensive flank till about 4.45 p.m., reinforcing the flank and using their rifles against the enemy whenever seen. A guard, formed by 'D' Company, 23rd Machine Gun Battalion had been posted on the Machine Gun Dump, and the Guard, realizing the situation, opened fire with two rifles while the other two men proceeded under Machine Gun and Rifle Fire to Lieutenant VIZARD and informed him of the situation.

1/4 Ox & Bucks LI

The enemy attack on the Ghelpac Fork was massive (seven battalions) and initially vigorous and well-conducted. The Ox & Bucks right forward company found themselves being bombed and machine-gunned from the rear, and formed a defensive flank. Despite also being heavily attacked from the front, rear and right flank, and under intense bombardment, it remained in contact with battalion headquarters. At 3.20 am GHQ ordered all outposts in. At 3.30 am this order was passed on just before all wires were cut, and wireless communication lost. The area on M. Lemerle occupied by brigade headquarters also housed the headquarters of 1/1 Bucks and of several artillery units, so was crowded with men, mules and command facilities, including the brigade wireless section. There was a particularly heavy enemy artillery barrage on this area, and many men sheltered in the OP tunnel. Unfortunately the wireless station was hit and put out of action so the brigade staff used runners, and liaison posts and patrols established by 1/1 Bucks, to contact battalions, and, when visibility allowed, signal lamps and semaphore to 143 Brigade and to divisional headquarters.

The picquets received the message at 4.30 am (no record of 'how', has been located) and attempted to comply despite having been bypassed by the enemy. The right picquet platoon of the Ox & Bucks regained the company position without difficulty but had to fight through the enemy to reach headquarters, where the platoon commander reported heavy enemy reinforcements heading towards the battalion's position from the north east. The platoon re-organized and returned to the line. The enemy were bombarding the area south of the Ghelpac bridge and the tunnel taking Prince's Road through the railway embankment. This bombardment may have been conforming to signal flares fired by the their leading echelons, as many accounts of the battle report almost constant use of 'signal lights' during the early part of the attack. The British SOS flares, on the other hand, either failed to ignite or did so at the bottom of their trajectory and well below the tree-tops. This, and the mist, dust and smoke, prevented SOS signals being seen by OPs on even nearby hills. However, some were seen by one or two Vickers posts of 48th Battalion MGC. The gun teams immediately opened fire on their SOS lines, or on targets of opportunity, either on Cunico Hill, or in the Holla re-entrant. Considerable numbers of the enemy were killed or wounded.

Hill 1021

Under cover of the barrage the enemy pushed the two Ox & Bucks forward companies, back towards Hill 1021, just forward of battalion headquarters. The commanding officer sent an SOS to brigade headquarters, then deployed HQ Company personnel into the line. Every man who could use a rifle - cook, servant, clerk, storeman - joined in, and their presence made all the difference. (This episode entered regimental lore as the 'Battle of the Cooks'). Around 10.30 am a counter-attack by a couple of platoons of the reserve company recovered the original front line trench but this had to be given up and a new line established along Roncalto Road. This was established at about 11.00 am, and re-inforced by D Company, 1/4 Royal Berks, which had arrived from Carriola and occupied Oxford Trench on the eastern slope of M. Lemerle, forming a back-stop for the Ox & Bucks around Hill 1021.

The left front Ox & Bucks company, less the left picquet platoon unable to retire through the enemy, withdrew as far as Pelly Cross, where Roncalto Road met Pine Avenue at Prince's Road. As the way south was guarded by 1/1 Bucks in Lemerle Switch and Poelderhook Trench, the company re-formed and rejoined the front line which curled round the north and eastern slopes of Hill 1021. The battalion now held a horse-shoe shaped line, comprising a series of improvised strongpoints with some hastily erected wire entanglements about thirty metres ahead of the shell-scrapes. On the right flank there was no contact with the 11/NF until much later in the day but fortunately the enemy did not press the attack in this section of the line. The left flank was in contact with 1/1 Bucks throughout the battle.

At around 5.00 pm a battered team of machine-gunners from D Company, 48th Bn MGC, arrived in the Ox & Bucks line near Pelly Cross. They had been manning the R7/R8 post on the extreme left of the battalion position, and after holding out all day fought their way to safety; unfortunately the guns were destroyed in the move.

The Battalion held their position around Hill 1021 throughout the afternoon and into the early hours of the morning, despite almost continuous machine-gun and rifle fire from the enemy. A steady shower of flares was fired close to the British line, either to help artillery observers establish the exact location of the front line or to illuminate any counter-attack. During the night brigade headquarters informed the battalion that 1/8 Worcesters would counter-attack through Pelly Cross towards the original front line west of Ghelpac Fork, starting at 4.30 am. This was in accordance with orders issued by General Fanshawe and was to take place in concert with an attack by 143 and 144 Brigades aimed at clearing the enemy from the woods between Prince's Road and the Cesuna Switch.

Reinforcements - 1/8 Worcesters

The 1/8 Worcesters had a difficult journey from M. Brusabo, due to traffic on Cavan Road, a detour round Handley Cross and wisps of gas lingering among hollows in the woods. The last stage from Handley Cross to Lemerle Switch was particularly arduous as it was made in complete darkness and along tracks obscured by smoke and mist, and littered with fallen trees and branches. The right companies deployed onto the start line at 4.25 am and immediately started their advance. The Worcester's Battle Narrative states that the companies 'found Ox & Bucks still holding out in front of them'. B Company advanced from Lemerle Switch towards the front line trenches and gained them without much opposition. The right hand platoon gained and cleared Pelly Trench with little difficulty, making contact with D Company 1/8 Worcesters on the left and 11/NF on the right. Enemy out-posts were spotted along Roncalto Road and in the village of that name. Patrols cleared these locations, as well as some out-posts on Durham Hill, and mounted a picquet there. A Company then occupied the trench to the left of B Company as far as the inter-battalion boundary at Ghelpac Fork. Around noon the battalion formally relieved the 1/4 Ox & Bucks, which withdrew into reserve at Carriola. They had sustained 176 casualties out of a reported strength of 552, which included flu cases on duty who were of limited operational value.

1/5 Gloucesters

The Battalion occupied a difficult position in the woods around Buco di Cesuna. The Battalion was so under-strength, 466 all ranks, that the brigade commander hesitated to place them in the front line. But there was no other unit readily to hand, so the Gloucesters did what

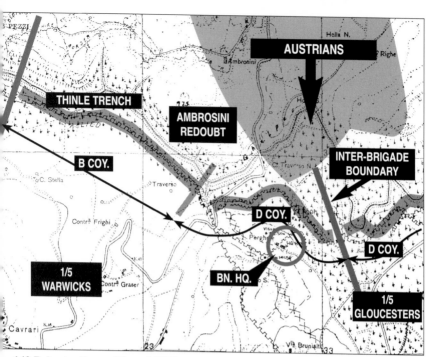

143 Brigade: the position of 1/5 Warwicks.

they could to man the sinuous line of trenches. The battalion bore the brunt of the Austrian attack, and suffered accordingly. The forward defences were breached but a stubborn defence blunted the enemy offensive.

Buco di Cesuna

The Battalion deployed two companies into the front-line: D (left) and B (right); A Company manned the picquets north of the Ghelpac, with a few remaining personnel strengthening the front line by battalion headquarters, near Buco di Cesuna. C Company was in support, spread out along Pine Avenue, about five hundred yards behind the front line. D Company had another 'D' Company, (1/5 Warwicks), on its left flank. The inter-battalion boundary was near the mouth of 'Happy Valley', just east of Perghele farm. At this point the line was very weakly held, with two or three infantry posts supported by R9 & R10 Vickers, D Coy, 48th Bn MGC. During the *Strafexpediton* the *k.u.k.* had crossed the river at that point, and retained detailed notes of the area, supplemented by good reconnaissance. The defence posts appear to have been specifically targeted by the enemy as they were almost destroyed during the preliminary barrage, during which heavy small-arms fire was also heard coming from that area. (The Battle Narrative of the Machine-

Gun Battalion refers to only one survivor of the Vickers post.) From the intensity of rifle and machine-gun fire reported from this area by observers in the British OPs, and later substantiated by patrols, the posts put up a desperate fight before being killed or captured. But the defences had been breached, and the enemy poured through the gaps in the wire.

Across the Ghelpac

The Austrians fanned out along and behind the front line. Some swarmed up onto Perghele Ridge where they attacked the defenders from the rear, while others started rolling-up the remnants of D Company to the east of the breach. The attack was delayed slightly when the second *k.u.k* wave was engaged by a platoon of C Company moving down Happy Valley to re-establish the picquet on Hill 972. The enemy were pushed back through the wire and went to ground along the river bank. A second platoon from C Company deployed onto the western side of Happy Valley to support their colleagues in D Company. By now the enemy were pouring back through the wire under cover of intense machine-gun fire coming from beyond the river, and from Perghele ridge.

143/145 Bde Boundary: penetration of front line at mouth of Happy Valley.

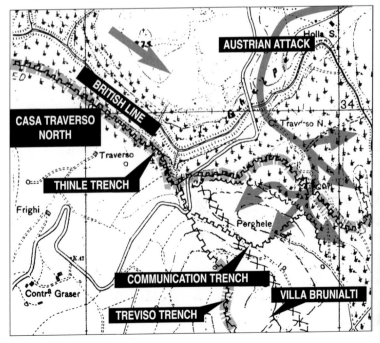

Into the woods

The Gloucesters were forced back into an 'S' shaped defensive line, then further back again. The Battalion, by now little more than two hundred effectives, fighting in two groups, was steadily pushed back behind Pine Avenue, until its back was on Lemerle Switch (see map on page 100). There the Gloucesters held their ground, but touch was lost between the groups. The right one entered the lines of 1/1 Bucks, and the tired troops had a brief rest, then regrouped and rearmed before returning to the fight. The left group made contact with the 1/8 Warwicks in Cesuna Switch, but remained in close contact with the enemy in the woods below M. Lemerle. The group had to make several more moves to avoid being encircled, but mounted a counter-attack which reached the main road. It was halted, and they were forced to withdraw yet again towards Lemerle Switch. The two groups of Gloucesters were eventually reunited and contact established on the right with the left company of 1/4 Royal Berks, and, on the left strengthened with the Warwicks in the Cesuna Switch. The Gloucesters remained in front of Lemerle Switch throughout the night, engaging the enemy whenever an opportunity presented itself, despite being under intense machine-gun fire, which fortunately was aimed too high to cause many casualties.

145 Brigade: maximum penetration by the enemy, midnight 15/16 June 1918.

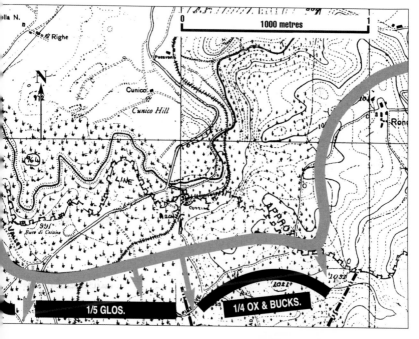

Reinforcements

Throughout 15 June more British troops were deployed into the line around the breach. Fanshawe ordered 144 Brigade to despatch 1/6 Gloucesters and 1/7 Worcesters into the fight. As mentioned earlier, in the early hours of 16 June the right wing of the 1/8 Worcester's counter-attack cleared the area in front of the Ox & Bucks. The remainder of 1/8 Worcesters formed up on Pine Avenue on the right of a counter-attack force comprising elements of 1/7 Worcesters, 1/4 Royal Berks, 1/6 Gloucesters and 1/7 Warwicks. The line extended from Prince's Road to Cesuna Switch, and from it troops swept forward at 7.30 am, clearing the remaining enemy from the pocket. In the centre and right little resistance was encountered. The ground was covered with dead and wounded Austrians, and littered with discarded or smashed weapons and equipment. The front line trench was cleared and garrisoned, and the out-post line re-established.

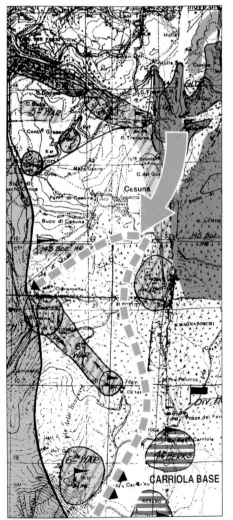

145 Brigade: intended *k.u.k* penetration routes through to supply dumps at Carriola and Campiello.

143 Brigade

The 1/5 Warwicks had a fighting strength of only 436 men, so the two companies in the front line had less than 200 bayonets to defend about 2,500 metres of trench. Fortunately the stretch of trench from the Canove road to the left divisional boundary, held by B Company, bordered the Ghelpac Gorge and was almost impregnable. But the stretch from the road to the mouth of Happy Valley was vulnerable to infiltration by the enemy as it twisted through forest, rocks, spurs, and was only manned with about 80 riflemen. A and C Companies were in depth, one around the farm buildings at Contrada Graser, the other further back in Cavrari. Battalion Headquarters was

104

scattered around Perghele, perched on an isolated spur, the Col del Vento (Windy Ridge), overlooking the Ghelpac. The headquarters staff were in several locations; Battle HQ occupied some dug-outs in rocks north of, and downhill from, the farm and about one hundred yards behind the front line trench and near the inter-battalion boundary. The Signal Office, one of a collection of battered huts, was nearby. The Battalion OP sat on the forward tip of the ridge with the Visual Signal Station behind it, with a good line of sight to the Brigade station on Hill 1152. The rest of Battalion Headquarters were in the remains of the farm buildings, with the cook-house in a re-entrant on the west side of the ridge, near the communication trench from the main road. 143rd Trench Mortar Battery had eight guns forward, five in the line (two with D Company, one with B and two behind Cesuna Switch), and three in reserve at Perghele. B Company, 48th Bn MGC, had twelve guns forward, including two covering the exit from Holla Valley. Various RFA and RGA batteries were in the brigade area in readiness for the Allied offensive.

First moves

The initial enemy barrage cut telephone lines and disrupted power-buzzer communication between 1/5 Warwicks and Brigade Headquarters, and as nothing could be seen from the Brigade Visual Signalling Station, the Brigade Intelligence Officer went forward to Perghele at 3.45 am to seek information. He took six Brigade Observers with him, and dropped them off at intervals along the route as a message relay, which worked satisfactorily until withdrawn later in the day. At 4.45 am the Brigade Commander received orders to man the Cesuna Switch, and these were passed to 1/6 and 1/8 Warwicks who reacted in accordance with the Defence Scheme: 1/6 moved forward to Brigade Headquarters and 1/8 into the Switch. The move of this latter battalion was particularly prompt as the runner bearing the message was intercepted by Captain A. Bridges, OC In-Lying Picquet Company (the duty company, waiting under arms at the Battalion position ready to act instantly in any emergency). Bridges acted immediately; the leading files passing Brigade Headquarters near the Val di Maso at 5.35 am. The company moved straight to the switch and at 6.30 am. reinforced the troops in Treviso Trench, which was then under machine-gun fire from the vicinity of Perghele.

1/5 Warwicks

The Austrian breakthrough into the mouth of Happy Valley rapidly overwhelmed D Company 1/5 Warwicks. The OC, Captain JB Florance, was captured before he could report the incursion, but fortunately the Battalion OP spotted the enemy advancing and notified Battalion Headquarters. At about 7.30 am the Visual Signalling Station was bombed and captured, and the explosions were spotted by the Brigade OP on Hill 1152 and immediately reported to an increasingly worried Brigade Commander. At Perghele, the Adjutant, Captain EPQ Carter MC, and the Intelligence Officer, Second-Lieutenant TL Goode, went to investigate but were quickly surrounded by the enemy, Carter being killed and Goode captured. At the same time the acting 2i/c, Captain WAP Watson MC, led a small counter-attack towards the gap in the front line, but was wounded. The acting CO, Major EAM Bindloss, led another party up-hill to re-capture the Visual Signal Station, the only means remaining for informing brigade headquarters of the situation. He was killed, rifle in hand, leading this sortie.

Perghele

The Battalion was now without any effective command or communication system, and the remaining three companies had to act on their own initiative. The remnants of Battalion Headquarters and

143 Brigade sector: HQ and D Company 1/5 Warwicks at Perghele overwhelmed.

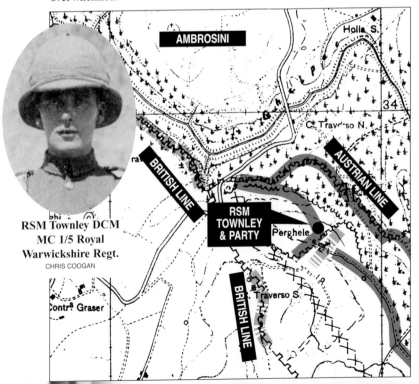

RSM Townley DCM MC 1/5 Royal Warwickshire Regt.
CHRIS COOGAN

Headquarters Company, a mere thirteen men - cooks, police, orderlies, clerks, plus one or two members of 48th Division Signal Company- were gathered up by the RSM, 24 year old Warrant-Officer Class I Frank Townley MC, and hustled into some huts at the eastern end of the farm. Here they conducted a vigorous defence, holding out for nearly four and a half hours until relieved. They accounted for ninety-one of the attackers and, of much more importance, they stopped the enemy from crossing the ridge where they could have got into the re-entrants below Perghele to destroy the Switch in relative peace. (RSM Townley was recommended for the VC but awarded the DCM.) This would have opened another attack route into Cesuna, and from there into the woods below M. Zovetto. Some Austrians did get past the make-shift strong-point by crawling down the communication trench towards the abandoned cook-house, but were caught in enfilade by a Lewis gun team firing from the ridge west of Villa Brunialti. Many of the enemy were killed, with most (if not all) of the survivors later succumbing to a bombing party from the 1/8 Warwicks.

Cesuna Switch

The two companies of 1/8 Warwicks in Cesuna Switch occupied Treviso Trench, which ran from C. Traverso South farm, through the grounds of Villa Brunialti (with a section in the house) and Guardiano (another farm, perched on a spur overlooking the Valle Gap), and across the gap itself. But with only about two hundred men to man the switch, there were few defenders, and the way was well-nigh open to the enemy.

The Brigade Intelligence Officer returned to headquarters at about 8.00 am and confirmed that a general attack was in progress around Perghele, information emphasized by the sound of intense rifle and machine-gun fire from various locations: Casa Traverso North (a 1/5 Warwicks outpost above the river bank), Buco di Cesuna and Perghele. OPs reported large parties of the enemy coming out of the woods west of Happy Valley and milling around Perghele, and others swarming out from assembly areas behind Cameron Trench in the redoubt at Ambrosini, and going down the slopes leading to the Ghelpac. Later, at 8.45 am, signal flares were seen in Happy Valley, which appeared to indicate the movement of troops towards Valle.

Holla Valley

The remaining companies of the 1/5 Warwicks did what they could to support their colleagues. B Company, holding the left thousand

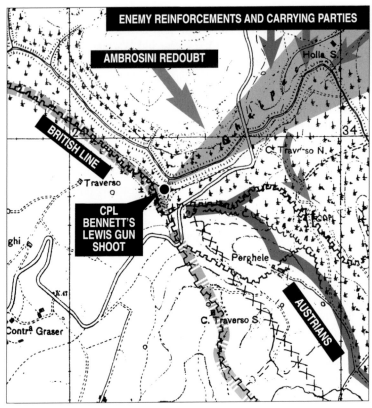

143 Brigade sector: defence of Perghele Ridge, and Cpl Bennett's Lewis Gun shoot.

metres of the front line, were relieved from guarding the last nine hundred metres by the 12th [Italian] Division taking it over. This was welcomed by Fanshawe, and B Company closed up to the right, and from a fairly safe stretch of trench commanded the Ghelpac Gorge as far as Holla South farm, and Holla Valley which was being used by *k.u.k* supply carriers, reinforcements and runners. The Warwicks poured Lewis gun fire and Stokes mortar bombs into this death-trap. Corporal H Bennett, Lewis gunner in 6 Platoon, fired 4,500 rounds (ninety-six magazines) in the course of the day. This accounted for untold numbers of the enemy and his actions earned him a Military Medal and, no doubt, the curses of his gun team who had to fill the magazines. B Company was also able to watch for any infiltration along the front line or down the communication trench from Perghele, and it was also available for counter-attack, as were A and C companies

108

who, on their own initiative, moved from Contrada Graser and Cavrari into Cesuna Switch.

Machine-gun and mortar support

The Left Section Vickers posts of B Company 48th Battalion MGC played an important role in holding the Austrian attacks. The L1-L10 guns all engaged the enemy throughout the day, firing initially on SOS lines until observed fire could be employed. The guns inflicted heavy losses on attackers coming down Holla valley, out of the Ambrosini redoubt, over Cunico Hill, or trying to cross Perghele ridge. L11 and L12 guns were covering the left flank and had no opportunity to fire.

Holding the Valle Gap

There was still a desperate shortage of defenders in the gaps in the wire below Valle. Here only a handful of sappers, Italian and British mortarmen, and gunners, some fighting as infantry while others manned some 18pdrs and 4.5-inch howitzers, mixed with some Gloucesters and men from 1/8 Warwicks, attempted to halt the enemy advance. Ammunition ran low, but supplies arrived, delivered almost into the front line by pack-mule. The enemy seized Casa Guardiano and opened fire with a machine gun, but this was knocked-out by a howitzer shell. The enemy still held the house, and Clo, and from these two places provided covering fire as their colleagues continued to advance. However, at around noon the enemy attack slowed, possibly because troops had discovered food and rum in the Gloucesters' Quartermaster's store. Whatever the reason, the *k.u.k.* attack was in its final throes, and the leading files did not get beyond the eastern outskirts of Valle.

1/7 Warwicks

General Fanshawe continued to deploy his reserves against the threat below Valle, having assessed that this was the critical point. The 1/7 Warwicks were ordered forward, and on arriving at the head of Happy Valley found enemy troops still advancing towards Valle. (The Warwicks had practised this very move twice in the days before the battle, rehearsing part of the Divisional Defence Plan.) Lieutenant-Colonel Knox, a vigorous and capable commander, reacted swiftly, and ordered the Battalion to fill the space between the Gloucesters backed against Lemerle Switch and the Warwicks in Cesuna Switch. The fire from the Battalion halted the offensive in this sector. The enemy troops took cover - and stayed there, content to do little more than spray their front with small-arms fire for hours on end.

Halting the offensive

Knox, however, was not content to let matters rest. He organized and led an attack on Guardiano and then Clo, killing, capturing or ejecting the defenders and manning the battered buildings with Lewis gun teams and riflemen. Knox also pushed a company northwards astride the switch until it emerged from the woods onto the pasture south of Perghele, opposite Villa Brunialti. Here it was stopped by machine-gun fire and snipers, and during this pause Knox was contacted by an officer of 1/6 Gloucesters who informed him of the counter-attack through the gap below Guardiano to clear the pocket between Lemerle and Cesuna Switches. The commanding officers agreed to combine forces. The counter-attack was planned to start at 6 pm. Two companies of each battalion stayed in the switch to hold the start line. The attack started on time but was held up by intense rifle and machine-gun fire, although the right-hand Gloucester company advanced nearly as far as Ghelpac Fork before being driven back. The 1/7 Worcesters now appeared in support on the right, and another attack was mounted at 8 pm, but after advancing for about three hundred yards, this stalled in the face of intense machine-gun fire. At about 9.30 pm a patrol of the 1/7 Worcesters made contact with the Ox & Bucks, near Pelly Cross, and so a line of sorts ran from Hill 1021 to Clo and Guardiano. The enemy had been contained, and made no serious attempt to advance, seeming content to create a defensive screen of intense machine-gun fire which was aimed too high to harm the British troops.

Final bout

143 Brigade: Cesuna Ridge and Casa Guardia. FRANCIS MACKAY

General Fanshawe ordered another attack for 4.30 am, and, as noted earlier, sent 1/8 Worcesters forward, supported by artillery, machine guns and trench mortars, with the guns concentrated on enemy supply routes north of the Ghelpac. This attack was launched on time, but by then the enemy were withdrawing. The Worcestershire Regimental history describes the scene:

> *At 4.30 a.m. the 1/8th Worcestershire advanced. A sharp fire met them at the outset; but the fierce night battle had done its work. The heart had been beaten out of the Austrian troops, and before the new attack their resistance collapsed. The Austrians were driven back in rout through the wood. Parties of the Gloucestershire, Royal Warwickshire and Royal Berkshire joined the Worcestershire battalions, and they swept forward through the woods in the grey light of dawn, recapturing the lost field guns and taking scores of prisoners. The old British front line was reached, and the fleeing enemy were hunted out into the open. Then the 1/7th Worcestershire halted to reorganize.*

Events on the right, (Ghelpac Fork) where there was little opposition, have been described, while on the left the enemy made a stubborn defence, which was probably a rear-guard action to cover the evacuation of wounded troops, of whom there were hundreds. At 7 am Fanshawe went forward and inspected the front just as a final attack was mounted to clear the pocket. The battalion commanders and their soldiers made one more effort, and the original line was restored by 8.15 am. The Austrians had again been stopped at M. Lemerle, as they had been exactly two years earlier, on 16 June 1916, during the *Strafexpedition*.

Chapter Seven

AFTERMATH

Recoil

The *k.u.k.* did not just withdraw from the woods of San Sisto and Buco di Cesuna. In many cases they withdrew far behind their own front line, leaving, at best, a few sentries in the trenches.

Hot pursuit

Immediately the front line was restored, the British re-occupied the picquet posts on Hills 972 and 1002, and cleared the woods on both sides of the Ghelpac, including the gorge to the east of the ruined bridge below Perghele; this sweep netted 100 Prisoners of War for the 1/6 and 1/7 Warwicks. The 1/6 then sent a strong patrol up to the Austrian redoubt at Ambrosini. They were not opposed, so penetrated the position and captured thirty prisoners and some machine guns. The 1/8 Worcesters also despatched patrols after the retreating enemy, and entered his front lines unopposed near Canove and took more prisoners. The patrols stayed in the enemy trenches, and reported their success to higher authority. The British had occupied, almost unopposed, a large portion of the enemy front line, which had been the objective of the cancelled Allied offensive. When news of this local success reached Lord Cavan he ordered both divisions to mount strong patrols with the aim of capturing the original objective line from Cima Tre Pezzi to Sec. Cavan and Graziani made urgent representations to General Diaz seeking permission to pursue the Austrians in force, but were refused, as there were no reserves to hand because of the fighting on the eastern end of the plateau and the Montello. This was a correct decision, as the British were still attempting to rectify the damage caused by the recent battle, and had not fully replenished their ammunition and supplies, neither had they repaired their defences or re-organized their guns and gun-positions, and supplying troops in what had been the enemy front line would also have been extremely difficult. Not only that, the Austrians had returned in force, and the advancing Allied patrols retired under heavy fire. Unable to advance, the British battalions cleared the battle area, buried the dead of both sides and repaired their defences.

The 1/8th Worcestershire had great captures to record:

120 unwounded prisoners, including two Austrian officers, 40

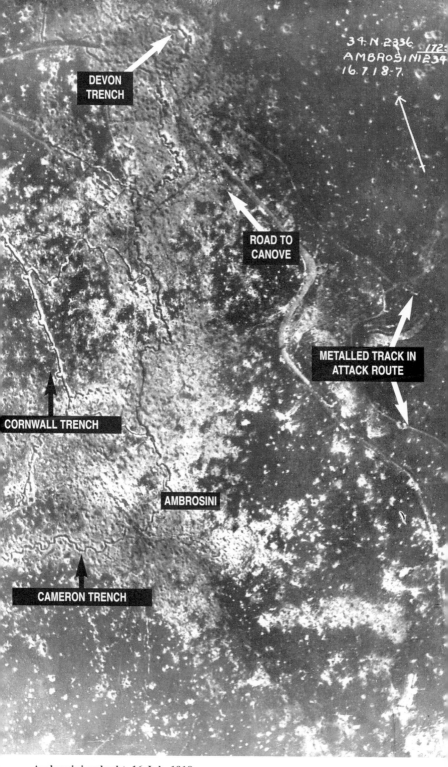

DEVON
TRENCH

34. N.2336 <u>172:</u>
AMBROSINI 234
16.7.18.7.

ROAD TO
CANOVE

METALLED TRACK IN
ATTACK ROUTE

CORNWALL TRENCH

AMBROSINI

CAMERON TRENCH

Ambrosini redoubt, 16 July 1918. WORCESTERSHIRE REGT COLLECTION.

wounded prisoners, 4 machine guns and 3 Flammenwerfers, besides the three mountain guns already mentioned. The prisoners consisted of various races, Austrians, Hungarians, Bosnians and Herzegovinians, and their antipathy towards each other was remarkable - they spat at each other, and unwounded prisoners would not carry a wounded one of another race on a stretcher until shown the business end of a bayonet by one of our escort. Two of the prisoners were Herzegovinian stretcher-bearers, over six feet tall, who, much to our surprise, were armed with enormous broad-swords, perhaps for the purpose of amputating a wounded limb! When the Prince of Wales called at the 1/8th Battalion H.Q. the following day he greatly admired one of these swords, but refused to accept it as a souvenir, as he said it rightly belonged to the C.O. of the Battalion.

The *k.u.k.* attack on the British Corps was defeated, and the Austrians thereafter largely stayed within their own lines until the Armistice.

The British remained on the plateau, and continued to raid the enemy, not always successfully. On 25 July 1918, much to their surprise, they were raided by the Austrians, and suffered casualties. In October the 23rd and 7th Divisions left the Sixth Army join the newly-formed Italian Tenth Army, commanded by Lord Cavan, on the Piave Front. The 48th Division remained in Sixth Army, and stayed on the plateau until the Armistice (4 November 1918 on this front). It fought in the final offensive in the northern mountains, where 143 Brigade conducted a successful attack up and over M. Moscaigh, a climb of over 2,500 feet. The Division claimed it was the first British formation to enter enemy territory in mainland Europe, crossing the Austrian frontier at the *Osteria del Termine* in the *Val d'Assa,* on 2 November 1918.

Assessment

The *k.u.k.* withdrew from the fight early in the morning of 16 June. The soldiers had tried to break the British lines, and failed. And yet there remains the unanswered question of why they failed to exploit their local successes at San Sisto, around Hill 1021, and in Happy Valley. The answer must lie with the Allied artillery, which shredded the follow-on forces as they struggled across the central plain. On the other hand, the *k.u.k.* artillery failed to pound the Valle choke-point, which could have allowed their infantry to penetrate deeper into the Allied forward zone. This failure to provide adequate fire-support was probably caused either by a break-down in the Austrian fire-control system - a lack of flares, inability to provide accurate targeting to the battery control posts, or destruction of Forward Observation teams as they tried to cross the central plain in the face of Allied artillery and indirect machine-gun fire.

The RAF was prevented by poor weather, and lack of accurate targeting information from Corps or Divisional Headquarters, from providing close air support or battlefield interdiction to the corps. The Austrian air service, the *Luftfahrttruppen,* did not appear in any strength over the plateau, so the need for counter-air operation was also limited. Therefore the RAF squadrons were tasked to support their Italian and French colleagues with attacking the Austrian bridgehead at the eastern end of the Montello, where *Feldmarschal* von Boroevic's attack across the Piave had made considerable headway.

By about mid-afternoon on 15 June the Trentino Group of Armies command echelon (Conrad) must have realized that the British and French lines were too tough to break, and that any *k.u.k.* force caught in the Allied rear areas could not be supplied from the Canove-Asiago front line. He decided to concentrate his forces against the Italians on the eastern end of the plateau, as the attack there was being mounted in concert with one even further east, on M. Grappa - which also failed.

Repercussions

The 48th Division's counter-attacks were conducted in accordance with a sound plan, carefully rehearsed, and well-executed by battalions winnowed by flu but manned by officers and men who were well trained, had high morale and who possessed, and felt confident to exercise, initiative on the battlefield. However, a few days after the battle, on 19th June, Fanshawe was relieved of command.

No reason was given for this. His dismissal may have been to placate the Italians, who ritually dismissed (*siluramente* - torpedoed) senior officers after a reverse on the field, and Lord Cavan was not a man to shirk politically inspired, if personally distasteful, decisions. Alternatively, Cavan may have decided that Fanshawe, once he had been briefed on the morning of 14 June on the possibility of an Austrian offensive, should have reinforced the front line with a battalion from 144 Brigade. Cavan may also have decided that the weakness of the defences around the entrance to Happy Valley, and at the Valle Gap, revealed a failure to identify the critical points of the front. (If so, he also seems to have missed it!) In addition, there are indications in the *Official History* that Fanshawe may have lost his grip on the battle during the critical phase on the morning of 15 June 1918. (He appears to have needed prompting to despatch a staff officer to find out what was happening at the breakthrough point.) Interestingly, Cavan visited Fanshawe at Carriola during the battle, and did not in any way comment or interfere with the arrangements in hand.

An additional factor was that artillery OPs of the Italian 12th Division, of X Corps, to the west of British, spotted the Austrians flooding over the Ghelpac early on the morning of 15 June. The Italian Corps commander, General Caviglia, was surprised by the apparent lack of response from the British, so ordered his artillery on M. Cengio to fire on the attackers. He later spoke with Cavan, who protested about Italian artillery fire falling on British positions. (How did he know it was Italian? Probably from British observers on M. Zovetto and M. Brusabo who would have been almost under the path of the incoming rounds hitting the area around the mouth of Happy Valley.) And, according to the Wilks' excellent book, General Caviglia was an acquaintance of Cavan's from pre-war years when they had been military attachés in Japan. Finally, given the parlous state of manning in the British Corps in Italy, let alone in the rest of the British army, any commander who allowed his forces to suffer unnecessary casualties would almost certainly be dismissed.

Fanshawe was well-liked and respected throughout the 48th Division. He trained his subordinate commanders thoroughly, and created a climate where they did not hesitate to use their initiative. Fanshawe wrote the Divisional Battle Narrative which is inadequate, inaccurate and trite, but it sheds no light on his sacking. He went uncomplainingly, gentlemanly to the end. Many officers in the division felt he had been shabbily treated, and complained for years afterwards. Captain Charles Carrington, 1/5 Warwicks, pursued the matter of Fanshawe's dismissal over nearly a quarter of a century, without apparently achieving any satisfaction. The general returned to Britain to command the second-line 69th (East Anglian) Division and did not see further active service. General Fanshawe died in 1946, aged 82, and is buried near Oxford.

There were casualties other than Fanshawe among the higher ranks. Conrad, who was without friends or influence at the Hapsburg court, was dismissed on 15 July 1918. He was placed on the retired list, and watched, impotent and anguished, as the *k.u.k,* and the Empire, disintegrated. After the war he lived for a while in Innsbruck, where he was on good terms with the officers of the Italian occupation force, then moved to Vienna. He died on 25 August 1925 and is buried in the

Hietzinger Cemetery, Vienna. There lies, as an Italian biographer gallantly put it, *l'ultimo grande condottiero della vecchia Austria imperiale* - the last Grand Captain of the old Austrian Empire.

Rewards

Emperor Karl received a Field-Marshal's baton, but not as planned in Padua, Vicenza, or even Italy. It was quietly handed over at a simple ceremony on 23 August 1918, his birthday, far from the front.

The remnants of the British front line battalions withdrew to the rear areas to rest and re-organize. The 1/5 Warwicks spent four days at Busibollo Camp, where they were visited by Lord Cavan. He inspected the ground where the breakthrough had occurred, and heard from RSM Townley the story of the defence of Perghele. The GOC was accompanied by the Prince of Wales, who later wrote of visiting the two divisions and one brigade; some accounts of the battle mention him meeting and talking with soldiers as he walked around the ground.

Italian Commemorative medal. DAVID HELMORE.

After the battle General Montuori, GOC Sixth Army had a commemorative medal struck for the battle. It is almost unknown to curators of regimental museums, and to medal collectors in Britain (and some in Italy!). It was made from silver, and had on the reverse a small continental-style security pin. The medals appear to have been struck in Milan by the firm 'Stefano Johnson'. The ribbon is very narrow, 1.5 cms, and woven in stripes, of uneven width, in red, white, green and blue. The medals were not engraved with the recipients name, and were delivered in small flat cardboard boxes. Some were issued to British officers who had taken part in the battle but do not appear to have been issued until after the Armistice. One letter of issue reads:

Lt AJ Jones

Herewith souvenir medal presented by General MONTUORI, Commanding 6th Italian Army, to British Officers in commemoration of the defeat of the Austrian attack on the ASIAGO Plateau, on the 15/16 June 1918.

117

Please acknowledge receipt.
(signature indecipherable)
Capt. and Adjt.
4.3.19   *1/7 Bn The Royal Warwickshire Regt*

Staying on

The Austrian offensive of June 1918 is referred to by the Italians as *il Quindici Giugno,* (the Fifteenth of June) without qualification by year. They mainly refer, of course, to the attacks on their defences at the eastern end of the Asiago plateau, on M. Grappa, and on the Montello, which in terms of size and ferocity completely overshadowed those in the British sector. The Italians are in no doubt that it was a climactic event, the turning point of their war. The army had redeemed itself after Caporetto, the *k.u.k.* had been defeated in open battle. Their way lay open for the final round of the campaign, what became known as the Battle of Vittorio Veneto, fought in the cold rains of autumn, beyond the Piave. In the central sector the assault river crossing was lead by the 2/1HAC and supported by the 1/Royal Welch Fusiliers; a feat of arms long forgotten at home.

But that lay in the future. On the plateau the British could take some pride in defeating a superior force in open battle, in unfamiliar surroundings, with forces weakened by disease, and with limited artillery support and few workable communications systems. It had indeed been a battalion commanders' and soldiers' battle, and fought in the mist and clouds.

View from the Montello looking towards the Asiago plateau, from the Canale Brentella at Crocetta Del Montello. TAYLOR LIBRARY.

Chapter Eight

TOURING THE BATTLEFIELD CAR TOUR 1.
Asiago, Sacrario Militare,
Monte Interotto

General

These tours are designed for both a tourist staying in Asiago, or visiting the plateau on a day-by-day basis from Verona or Venice. No precise time for each tour is offered, as everyone has their own interests, pace and schedule, but most should occupy a half-day.

Getting there: A - from the Venetian Plain

Starting at Venice, Verona or Vicenza, on the A4/E70 *Serenissima Autostrada* (Milan - Venice). Find and enter the A31 *Valdastico,* head north for Asiago. As you near the escarpment the road to Asiago will be seen winding upwards; don't worry as it is excellent. At the end of the A31 join the S349 and head for Asiago. Remember the infantrymen who ascended by foot! Continue along the S349, and at the bridge over the Astico, look out for the ornate grenades on the bridge portals; they commemorate the Sardinian Grenadier Brigade, which defended, at horrific cost, one of the nearby peaks during the Great War. Follow the road

Hair-pin bends on the *Strada di Costo*, M Pau above.
FRANCIS MACKAY

Campiello 1918. VITTORIO CORA.

upwards as it winds in to a series of ten hair-pin bends, numbered. Just after *Turnante* 5 there is a lay-by on the right, pull in and stretch your legs. Above you is M. Pau, and on the right, as you face the escarpment, a balustrade. This is the remains of a bridge over the rack railway. The road, *il Strada Costo,* named for the slope below M. Pau, follows the approximate line of the

Campiello Station, 1998. FRANCIS MACKAY

Great War supply route from dumps in Chiuppano and Caltrano foothills. Two long-established cafes, The *Café Barricata* at the bottom, and the *Osteria Barricata* at the top, were in 1918 welcome watering stops for mules and men. Carry on up the road. In summer be alert for the shadows of para-gliders suddenly appearing on the windscreen, and at week-ends beware of motor-cyclists roaring up and down the hills, usually in threes, all trying to beat the bogey time between the cafes.

Unhappy Valley

You are now entering the upper reaches of the *Val Canaglia,* and soon reach the disused railway station at Campiello. In 1918 this was the railhead for a vast Allied stores dump in what was called Unhappy Valley. The restored station is now a holiday home. The inn opposite the station serves good food (home-made salami, polenta, Asiago cheese) but the offices are primitive. The road on the left of the inn leads to M. Cengio, where the Sardinians fought so tenaciously: a fascinating battleground which has nothing to do with the events described in this book, however!

Beside the station is a huge cistern, built to supply railway engines but also used during the Great War by troops garrisoned in Unhappy Valley. The railway track from Campiello to Asiago is now a footpath. To the right of the station is a forest track: in 1918 this was Connaught Road, the supply route to Carriola. It is not suitable for cars.

Ghelpac gorge

Drive on and follow the signs for Asiago through the village of Tresche-Conca. As the road starts to descend towards the central plain look to the left for a large house, behind some railings, with a sign indicating *Museo delle Cuchi* (pottery whistles): it was the site of a forward ammunition dump used by B Company 48th Bn MGC during the battle of 15/16 June 1918. At the left-hand bend, you should catch a glimpse of a massive white monument at your one o'clock. That is the *Sacrario Militare,* in Asiago. Carry on down the slope and through the bends. If possible, about a hundred yards before the road enters the woods, take a quick glance at the ridge to the west. On the morning of 15 June 1918 Contrada Frighi and Casa Traverso West housed the rear companies of 1/5 Warwicks. From the ground between the houses

Cavari - *Contrada* Frighi: support positions 1/5 Warwicks, 14/15 June 1918.
FRANCIS MACKAY

An Italian 7.7cm Howitzer outside Canove station, now a museum. MUSEO DELLA GUERRA, CANOVE.

Vickers guns of the left sections, A Coy 48th Battalion MGC fired over 24,000 rounds in support of 143 Brigade during the battle. Once in the shelter of the trees the road descends into the Ghelpac Gorge; there is a sharp left turn over the bridge. Just before crossing the river note the quarry workings on the right: they have obliterated most of the trenches below Perghele. As the road swings left to cross the bridge a quick glimpse on the right can be obtained of Holla Valley, scene of the slaughter of *k.u.k. Materialtruppen* by Stokes bombs and Corporal Bennett's Lewis gun. As the road climbs away from the river, glance into the small valley on the right, this was part of the western attack route used by the *k.u.k.* during the offensive. Ambrosini, the 1918 *k.u.k.* redoubt, and jumping-off point for one wave of the attack into Happy Valley, now a cattle-rearing centre, lies just over the hill above you. Head through Canove (note the location of the war museum) and follow the road round to the right to reach Asiago.

Asiago - restored station. FRANCIS MACKAY

Asiago

Just beyond the very obvious cheese-factory between Canove and Asiago, is a car and coach park, but try to get into the town proper to park. At the first crossroads in the town turn right for the car-park next to the old station building. The tourist office in the restored station building can provide a Great War map of the plateau *(Luoghi della Grande Guerra 1915-1918).*

Getting there: B - from the Brenner Pass

Follow the A22/E45 Modena-Brenner Autostrada to Trento, and then follow the signs to Lavarone, Vezzena and Asiago, which lies 55 kms from Trento - along a winding road through beautiful scenery. The road enters Asiago opposite the station car-park.

Asiago Town

A good introduction to the town, the plateau and the battle can be obtained from the *Sacrario Militare.* Be aware that it closes every day at about noon for about two hours, as do many public buildings in Italy, including some tourist offices in the quiet months.

The town was destroyed in the Great War, but carefully restored in the 1920s. It is a very pleasant place, whether for strolling, sightseeing, staying or people-watching. Eating and drinking places abound, so lunch, coffee and a snack, or picnic supplies are readily available (Mondays excepted), as Asiago is a popular resort, winter and summer. There are several excellent book-shops, all featuring a good range of publications and videos about the Great War; the Italian text is surprisingly easy to follow, and the books reasonably priced. One of the most interesting of these shops is that of Sr Bonomi, just off the main square, behind the fountain. [Sr Bonomi not only sells many books about the Great War, but has published two about local railways, one on the rack-and pinion line which ran to Asiago, the other about wool trains in the Val d'Astico. Both contain photographs and text about the role of these railways in the Great War.]

The side-streets contain many fascinating small shops and cafes, but few have staff with any command of English. The people are very pleasant and helpful and although no-one seems in a hurry, everything works.

Sacrario Militare. FRANCIS MACKAY

Sacrario Militare

The memorial is at the top of a long avenue which is steeper than it looks. (There is a car-park at the bottom, and an overflow one is available in a nearby field at peak times. The period around

123

Asiago, view over No Man's Land from the Play Park; Malga Fassa pasture in distance. FRANCIS MACKAY

14-16 June, when the defeat of the 1916 *Strafexpediton* is commemorated, is especially hectic in Asiago and Cesuna.) The memorial is manned by helpful young *Alpini,* very shy with foreigners. The exterior is typical of monuments of the Fascisti/Mussolini era:

View from M. Interotto, one time *k.u.k.* op. VITTORIO CORA

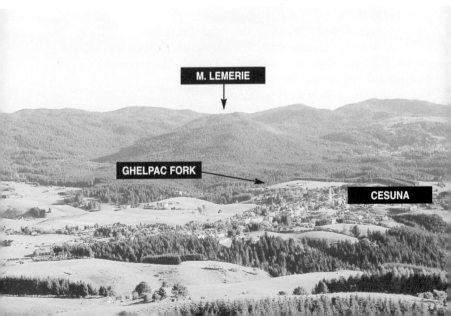

massive, solid and impressive. The interior is dark, brooding and sobering, as the walls contain the bones of 54,000 Italian and Austro-Hungarian soldiers, some named, some *ignoto*. Brochures are available, but none - so far - in English. There is a small collection of militaria, including some British items, and a three-dimensional map, a *plastiche*, explaining the phases of the fighting on the plateau and the immediate area from 1915 until the Armistice on 4 November 1918. There are some photographs of British troops, including one of the Prince of Wales with an escort from the Northamptonshire Dragoons. In the centre of the mausoleum is a simple chapel, with various corps or regimental memorials, including one from an Austrian ex-servicemen's association.

The battlefield

Go out of the mausoleum and up onto the esplanade. Turn and look across the avenue to the west. The steep hills on your right housed the Austrians, and the low wooded ones on the left the Allies. The Austrian front line ran through the town to Canove, following the line of the railway. Imagine the problems facing the *k.u.k.* in attempting to move supplies across the open slopes seen on the right. The British sector ran from your nine o'clock as far as the last visible ridge at your eleven o'clock.

The wooded park, the *Parco Giochi* [Play Park] behind the station is an excellent picnic site. Take your ease among the trees, and study the scenery to the south. Much of the area in front was No Man's Land; the British front line was just inside the forest.

M. Interotto - *k.u.k.* OP.

It is worth taking a few minutes to drive to M. Interotto to see No Man's Land and the British sector from a *k.u.k.* OP. Drive back to Canove. Continue on to Canove but bear right at the first cross-roads, and head for Camporovere. In the village, turn right at the T-junction, and then left just before the fork in the road. Drive up to any convenient point before the edge of the forest and look out over the central plain. Reflect again on the problems of re-supply, observation and fire-control. The summit above this location is M. Moscaigh, site of 'Archibald', the *k.u.k.* searchlight bombarded by Hugh Dalton's howitzer in the early hours of 15 June 1918. Return to the village and turn left for the car tour to Granezza, the walks to San Sisto Ridge and Canove, or right for the car tours of Ghelpac Fork, and the Cesuna area.

View from Sacrario Militare, looking west, over Asiago town. FRANCIS MACKAY

WALK 1:
San Sisto Ridge-Asiago
About 8kms; 3 hours, including exploration

The starting point is Asiago station. **(S)** Stand in front of the station building facing the Sacrario Militare, and walk down the street to the right, the *Vialle Giuseppe Garibaldi*. Go down the street, turn right into the *Via Cavour*, go straight ahead when it becomes the *Via San Carlo*, then right into the *Via Don Viero*. Go along that road into the country, passing *Contrada* Ave, **(1)** a cluster of houses on Ave Spur, to the right. In 1918 it was a *k.u.k* redoubt and, like Ambrosini, an assembly area

Walk to San Sisto Ridge.

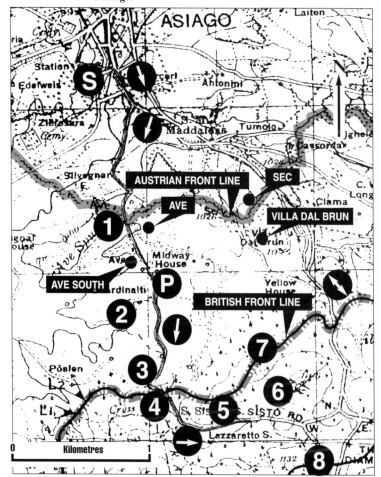

NOTE: The map used for the car and walking tours are based on a copy of a 1918 one, found in Italy in 1993. It is obviously a copy of a British original. The 'Brit-Cem'y' - British cemeteries marked on the maps were relocated in the 1920's.

San Sisto Ridge. View of Picquet and Vickers R3 positions. FRANCIS MACKAY

and jumping-off point for the attack on the British, in this case, San Sisto Ridge. The redoubt was protected by a belt of wire, with patrol gaps used by the attacking troops to enter No Man's Land. The redoubt was connected to the Austrian front line by the *Tranchee de Bataille;* no British name has been located for this stretch of communications trench, but it was an extension of Norfolk Trench, which ran eastwards from a *k.u.k.* support area near a ruined farm called Moselle (see Walk **2**). The trench was to be a French objective in the intended Allied June Offensive.

San Sisto Ridge can be seen straight ahead, a barely discernible whale-back of trees against the forested slopes of Prinele ridge. Note

Poslen from the Ave-San Sisto track. FRANCIS MACKAY

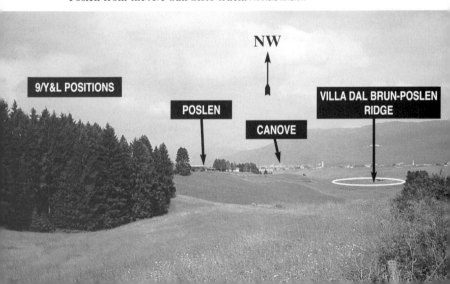

the broken ground on either side of the road which provided ideal cover for infiltraters, and for outposts and picquet positions. Next, on the right at the top of the rise, is Ave South, the site of a British outpost position. The next ridge, marked Perghele on modern maps, runs from the Villa Dal Brun to Poslen. Guardinalti **(2)** farm, sometimes used by the *k.u.k.* as listening post, is to the right. It overlooks a rocky slope, *Scogli de Ave,* the site of another British outpost.

The road now becomes a very rough track, which leads into the forest. At the top of the last rise before the forest, turn round and look northeast at the ground over which the *k.u.k.* attacked in the early hours of 15 June 1918; it has changed little in eighty-one years! At the same point a track runs off to the west to Poslen. That *k.u.k.* redoubt was very close to the British front line; it was connected by Coldstream Trench to dead ground around the hamlet of Roncalto and the main enemy line (Oxfordshire Trench) by footpaths. This track makes a pleasant little detour enabling you to see the ground across which the *k.u.k.* assault troops advanced towards the trenches held by 9/Y&L. The mounds **(3)** where Vickers R3 and R4 were sited are near this track junction.

9/Y&L positions

Continue up the track into the Glen and at the edge of the forest a right turn leads into the Y&L position. **(4)** A brief search in the undergrowth will reveal the remains of trenches, machine-gun pits and communication trenches, about fifty yards back from the edge of the trees. The main trench line can be followed for some distance to the west before it peters out. In the same way one of the communication trenches can be followed uphill, towards the site of the Malga Fassa Switch and strong-point. The battalion headquarters was at the bottom of the pasture, still used by a dairy farmer; signs prohibit entry.

San Sisto Ridge

From the point where the track enters the forest - walk up the track

San Sisto chapel and track to ridge-top paths and trenches. FRANCIS MACKAY

CHAPEL

TRACK

San Sisto Ridge: entrance to Italian dug-out.

as it climbs up through a small glen until a clearing and track junction appears. The large blocks of red stone on the left are the remains of recent quarrying at the western end of the ridge and are there to keep the unwary from danger. Bear left and go into San Sisto Valley. Continue along the track into the pasture; the chapel **(5)** appears on your left and is worth a quick visit. Next to it, on the right, is a flat mound, the remains of an earlier chapel, damaged during the Great War. The Italian war cemetery mentioned by Hugh Dalton, and illustrated in his book, was to the south of the road, among the trees. To the right of the chapel a track leads up to the ridge-top. If ascending, note, at the start of the track, low down on the right-hand side, the entrance to a dug-out. Lieutenant-Colonel Knox, Commanding Officer of the 1/7 Warwicks, was killed in this area by a direct hit on a similar bunker, probably by a 305mm howitzer shell, on 23 September 1918. Hudson's Battle Headquarters was probably near the bottom of the track, and you are close to the scene of his counter-attack.

Go up the track to the crest of the ridge, and on the paths made by hunters and walkers work your way along the crest towards the east, and the remains of the trenches held by C Company will appear. Follow them for about two hundred yards, noting the mortar bays and *tana di volpe,* until a prominent track appears **(6)** on the right, coming up from the valley. Turn away from the clearing and work your way down the slope, bearing gently left. The remains of a communication trench can be found and followed to the bottom of the slope into the remnants of the front line. The communication trench is not continuous, possibly due to the effects of logging over the years, but bits of wire entanglements can still be seen: keep clear!

The front line trench is shallow, damp and full of boulders, and, in some places bits of barbed wire, old cans and broken bottles. Note the lack of traverses. It was a series of 'runs'; difficult to defend, even with plenty of troops. The exact spot where Edward Brittain was killed is open to conjecture but the spot **(7)** marked on the map is deduced from the scant evidence available at the time of writing.

From the front line trench move forward to the track running just inside the wood. Work your way along the track and trench to the right, following the latter round the slope of Hill 1106 towards the main road, which in 1918 was the boundary with the French sector. A Company headquarters was at the extreme end of the trench, close to where the 1000 metre (tourist board map) contour curves south to the main road. The road was re-aligned in the Sixties, and is now closer to Hill 1106 than it was in 1918.

To return to Asiago, either walk along the (narrow) main road, or re-trace your steps to the ridge and explore the valley, especially the virtually intact line of Adelphi Trench. **(8)** To return to Asiago, two options are available. One; find the track leading down from the ridge and follow it through the woods, past the hospital (which has traces of the Villa Dal Brun incorporated into its structure) and the farm at Sec and onto the main road. Two: retrace the route past the chapel and down the glen and past Guardinalti, etc. On reaching the first group of houses on the right, **(P)** some recently-built holiday homes, look left and note the massif to the west. This includes M. Pasubio, another battlefield worth visiting, but with no British connections. Return to the station car-park and have a good strong glass of ... water.

San Sisto Ridge: ridge-top trenches. FRANCIS MACKAY

WALK 2:
The Austrian Front Line and Canove Museum
About 6-8kms; 3 hours depending on return route.

Start at Asiago station. **(S)** and follow the railway path **(1)** into open country by the new car-park. **(2)** The front line (Norfolk Trench, crossing *Edelweiss* Spur, named after the still-extant *Albergo* of that name) ran slightly to the south (over the rise) of the railway path but joined it just beyond the cheese factory, at the top of *Coda Spur*. Still by the car-park: to the west can be seen, from left to right, Casello No.8, a railway cutting, a cluster of houses amongst trees (once the site of Gaiga South), and to the right at the bend in the road, Gaiga North.

Walk down the railway path, and descend to, and round, the cheese factory. In 1918 the area around the factory was a busy *k.u.k.* forward base. Opposite the factory is Mosele, **(3)** once a battalion headquarters. This whole area was vital for the Austrians, with supply points, troop shelters, mortar positions, headquarters, and, in June 1918, assembly areas and jumping-off points for forces attacking the British. Beyond the factory, and just before the bend in the road, note the embankment. This was a railway branch line, built in 1916, to move supplies to Camporovere, for passage to Italian mountain defences. The *k.u.k.* used the track-bed to move supplies by hand-cart, mule train and lorry, at night or in mist. Ambulances also used it during the night, and, occasionally, by day. In the cutting below Gaiga South, **(4)** beyond

Walk to Canove.

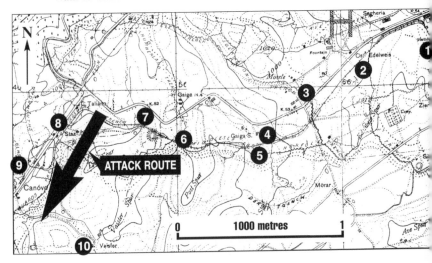

K.u.k. front line and redoubts west of Asiago. FRANCIS MACKAY

Aerial photo of embankment, Casselo No. 9, Moselle, Giaga South and North, and supply area. WORCESTERSHIRE REGT COLLECTION.

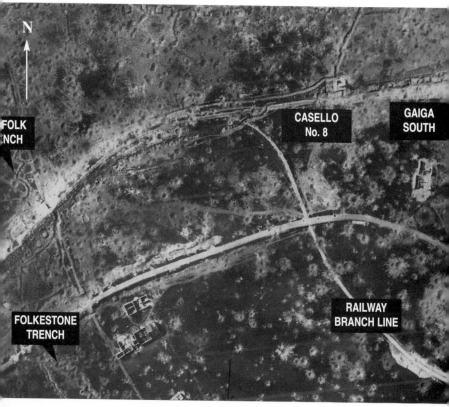

Remains of narrow-gauge railway branch line to Camporovere.
FRANCIS MACKAY

Casello No.8, there is a dugout entrance, **(5)** at ground level on the south side. There are more dugouts further along the track but sealed off as they attract rubbish-dumpers, dogs and children. In 1918 the cutting was lined with burrows, shelters and dug-outs, and was the target for several large trench raids by the British, not all of them successful; on one occasion the raiding party was 'seen off' by Bosnian infantry.

Continue along the railway path towards Canove. Note how Cima de Fonte and M. Lemerle can be seen from many points **(6)** (photo page 135) along the line and imagine the superb view British observers would have enjoyed of the Austrian front line and communication trenches. Also clearly visible are the rolling pastures of No Man's Land.

On the outskirts of Canove, as the line bears left, look left, (photo page 135) and down **(7)** into the shallow valley. This was the start of the 'assault route' which followed the valley from below the C. *Taliano* and west of Little Spur, down to the Ghelpac. Modern maps show a stream but the gully only contains water after a heavy and prolonged snow fall, a rare occurence in recent years.

Continue along the track and past the swimming pool and into what was once the railway goods yard but is now a car-park. The small stone building to your front is the old

Railway cutting, west of Casello N 8, site of *k.u.k.* dug-outs in 191
FRANCIS MACKAY

View of Cima di Fonte and M. Lemerle from railway track, looking past Vaister farm.

railway goods shed, now the meeting room of the local branch of the *Alpini* Regimental Association; if invited in for a slight refreshment don't expect to get out in a hurry! Next is the splendid old station, **(8)** now home to the *Museo Storico della Guerra 1915-18*. It is full of interesting items, including a fascinating piece of electrical equipment for treating wounds and infection with ultra-voilet radiation. It consists of a hand grip, with power-cables, and a series of odd-shaped glass tubes, containing filaments, which plug into the grip, for treating various wounds or parts of the body. This display has only a small caption, and cries out for more information. A new wing was added in 1998, and houses some interesting vehicles and a few British cap badges (some inappropriate) and medals.

The museum is open daily between 1 July and the second Sunday in September: the hours are 10.00-12.00 and 15.00-19.00. Outside those dates ask at the Roxy Bar for Signor Franceso Magnaboschi (or telephone 0424 692405) and he will open the premises. There is a small entrance fee, and a modest display of books. The background music is of traditional *Alpini* songs.

The Café Panda, opposite the museum, serves excellent ice-cream, snacks, home-baked pastries and (of course) good coffee. There are

Start of attack route leading Ghelpac Fork, looking south west from railway path. FRANCIS MACKAY

several good restaurants and delicatessen in the village, and the museum has a garden with picnic tables, overlooking Little Spur and the gully leading to Ghelpac Fork.

Options

Either re-trace your steps, or return to Asiago via No Man's Land. Whichever route you decide on, take a few minutes to walk down the main road to the first car-park, and go to the far side. There is a good view **(9)** of the Val d'Assa. In 1918 the gully below Canove was lined with dugouts and communication trenches. It was used as an assembly area for many of the *k.u.k.* assault units and follow-on forces on June 1918.

Return to the station and either retrace your steps to Asiago, or return via No Man's Land. Head south on the railway path until it

Canove Museum. The old Booking Office, Museo Di Guerra, Canove.

crosses a secondary road. Turn left along the road until it crosses **(10)** what was Vaister Spur and intersects a farm track. Turn and look back towards the village and you can see the ground crossed by the Ox & Bucks 'snatch' patrol on the night of 15 June 1918. Do not go down (right) the short stretch of track to Waister farm (current spelling) as there is constant movement of farm vehicles. You can either return to the railway path, or carry on down the secondary road and back to Asiago by the Ghelpac valley, scene of night patrols by both sides.

CAR TOUR 2:
Barental, Granezza, Tattenham Corner
About 22kms, 4 hours.

From Asiago station car-park **(S)**, follow the directions for Walk 1 but continue on the Via San Carlo and turn right onto the main road for Bassano del Grappa. After about 1.5 kms, just beyond the road into the hospital, turn right **(1)** into the forest and follow the main track as it swings left. Bear right at the next fork (watch for the CWGC signs) and you are on what was Barental Road. After about 150 metres, look for a concrete barbecue stand **(2)** on the right. Park; within a few yards is the eastern end of Adelphi Trench. The trench is very rocky but can be followed to San Sisto Ridge. (If you decide to follow the trench it is best to walk alongside it, and even then take your stick. Once at San Sisto Ridge, go to the chapel and follow the notes for Walk 1 from that point.)

Return to the car, and continue up Barental Road.

The first track on the right leads to San Sisto Ridge, note this for later. Carry on along Barental Road, and after about 300 metres start looking on the right for a red-and white painted rock **(3)** in the undergrowth. This is marked *Ospedaletti* on modern maps and marks the site of a Great War Italian underground hospital; a hole in the bank beyond indicates one of the entrances. Carry on for about 50 metres, on the right are some concrete ruins **(4)**, like Nissen huts. They may have been used by British support units, and are marked on modern maps as *Ospedaletti Inglesi*.

NOTE: The maps date from 1918, with some road changes added. The British cemeteries were consolidated in the 1920s; only Cavaletto is on the original site. The trench lines are approximations only.

North section.

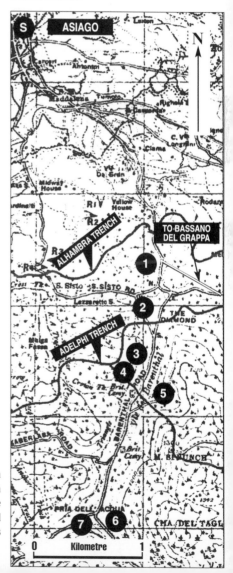

Adelphi Trench, by the Barental Road. FRANCIS MACKAY

Barental Road; marker for the site of Italian underground hospital. FRANCIS MA

The next place of interest is Barental Cemetery **(5)** which contains many of the dead from the fighting on 15/16 June 1918, brought here when the dead in earlier cemeteries were exhumed and re-interred at this quiet location, under the pines. Further details are given in Car Tour 3, below.

Pria dell'Acqua

Proceed another 500 metres to the cross-roads and *rifugio* at Pria dell'Acqua, **(6)** once the site of Italian barracks, and an Allied supply point. Hugh Dalton's battery was positioned in the woods to the right, (west) with one gun sixty metres **(7)** from the cross-roads. Opposite the rifugio are some dug-outs and a set of enigmatic concrete foundations, possibly the base of the pumping engine for the *impianti idrici,* as there

Barental Road: 'Ospedaletti Inglesi'. FRANCIS MACKAY

Barental Cemetery. FRANCIS MACKAY

Pria dell'Acqua, from Langabissa Road. FRANCIS MACKAY

was a *serbatoio* (reservoir) and water distribution point nearby, or the base-station of a *teleferiche,* although none are marked at that location on Italian army engineer maps of 1918. There are here two Second World War memorials to partisans.

In 1918 the road to the south of the crossroads, Pria dell'Acqua Road, was the main British supply route from Granezza and the plains and was always busy. It is much quieter now, except during August, but the occasional timber lorry makes driving interesting at times, especially when there is snow or ice on the track. Cows are another hazard, so if weather allows drive with the window open and one ear cocked for their bells.

Granezza (*Valle Granezza di Asiago*)

Continue up the main road and after two kms or so the *Osteria di Granezza* (7) appears on the right, just after a large memorial to partisans from the Setti Commune killed during the Second World War (there is one English name, Major Wilkinson, an SOE Team Leader, killed in 1945). The *Osteria* is a good place to eat but is open only in the summer. The pasture area to the south was once thronged with huts and hard-standings, but nowadays is inhabited only by cows and

Pria dell'Acqua, 1917 Italian barracks, later occupied by British troops.

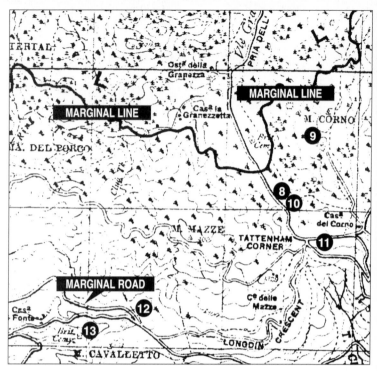

Southern section.

ponies. Proceed along the road; next on the right is a *malga,* (a seasonal mountain dairy where cheese-making is carried on) and, opposite, another *osteria* where coffee, light refreshments, cheese, butter and salami are usually available in the summer.

Edward Brittain's grave. FRANCIS MACKAY

Granezza CWGC Cemetery

This **(8)** lies at the southern end of the pasture. Keep a sharp look-out on your left, as it is set a little way back from the road on the left-hand side. Watch for the *back* of the CWGC sign; most visitors are expected to arrive from the south, by way of the mountain road from Lugo di Vicenza.

Park carefully as the road is used all year. Captain Edward Brittain's grave is on the left, Plot 1, Row B, Grave 1. In the summer months it is frequently garnished with bouquets. During the period 1994-1999 all of the CWGC cemeteries on the plateau were visited on, or near, Armistice Day by British and Allied personnel from the NATO airbase in Vicenza. Poppies or wreaths were laid, the Two Minute Silence observed, and 'For the Fallen' recited.

Granezza pasture and Malga.

A footpath at the side of the cemetery leads to some restored Italian trenches, on the flank of M. Corno. **(9)** This was part of the Marginal Line, the last defence line before the escarpment. The line can be traced, with some difficulty, east to the cliffs above the Brenta, and west to M. Pau. [Not recommended for the casual explorer, as the

Granezza Cemetery.

forest is very thick in places, and a solitary walker can easily become lost.]

Lieutenant Colonel Knox/143 Brigade memorial

A few yards to the south of the cemetery, on the same side of the road, is the family memorial **(10)** to Lieutenant-Colonel JM Knox DSO, and the officers, NCOs and men of 143 (Warwickshire) Brigade, who fell on the Asiago plateau in 1918. The brigade spent about eight months on the plateau in 1918, from March until November, with an occasional short rest in the Val d'Agno. The memorial is described in greater detail in the Cemeteries and Memorials section below.

Memorial to Lt Col Knox and the men of 143 Brigade Memorial.

Tattenham Corner

Drive on past a cluster of buildings (ski-tows, cafe, huts) to a cross-roads, and into the car-park of the *Rifugio Monte Corno*. This was Tattenham Corner. **(11)** The views over the Venetian Plain are stunning, and the *Rifugio* serves good wholesome food; but it is busy in high summer, and at week-ends.

Cavaletto Cemetery (13)

This lies about fifteen minutes drive from Tattenham Corner, just off the war-road (Longdin Crescent) to the foothills. During July and

Cavaletto Cemetery. FRANCIS MACKAY

August it is better to park at the junction **(12)** with what was Longdin Crescent, and walk down to the cemetery. This cemetery lies about five hundred metres off the road, at the bottom of a hollow, and is almost out of sight of cars. A rough track leads down to the gates, but walk carefully as the rocky bed can be slippery after rain. If driving down from Longdin Crescent, be warned that turning a car is difficult on the narrow and twisting mountain road, and may involve travelling some distance. The road (eventually) reaches the foothill villages of Fara, Calvene and Lugo di Vicenza, which in 1918 housed British supply dumps, service schools and support units. There are good connections from Lugo to the A31 for Vicenza, Padua and Verona.

Note! Longdin Crescent leads to the Marginal Road, skirting the Escarpment to M. Pau/Carriola, it is **unsuitable** for cars.

CAR AND WALKING TOUR 3:
The Battle in the Woods (A)
145 Brigade,
Ghelpac Fork, Hill 1021, Boscon, Handley Cross

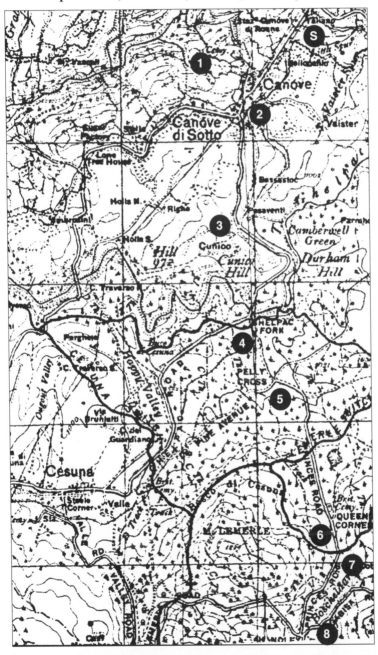

About 10 kms, 3 hours, to Handley Cross and back.

General.

Start at Canove museum car park. **(S)** Turn left and note, between the houses on the right, the deep and unexpected drop **(1)** into the Val d'Assa, where the *k.u.k.* had many dumps and shelters carved into the side of the ravine. [See also photo on page 95] Drive for about 800 metres and take the main road on the left **(2)**. This turn can be tricky as traffic from the right is obscured. Proceed; after about two kilometres Cunico Hill **(3)** will appear on the right and the railway path will appear in the valley on the left, below what was Camberwell Green.

Ghelpac Fork (4)

The picnic and car-park **(4A)** were built in 1995 and occupy what

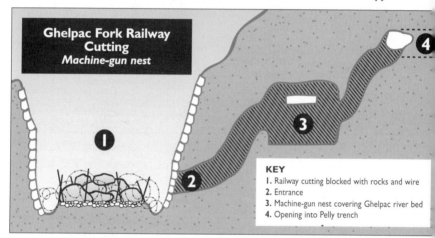

Ghelpac Fork Railway Cutting
Machine-gun nest

1

2

3

4

KEY
1. Railway cutting blocked with rocks and wire
2. Entrance
3. Machine-gun nest covering Ghelpac river bed
4. Opening into Pelly trench

Ghelpac Fork: entrance to Machine Gun post, railway cutting (See page 146).

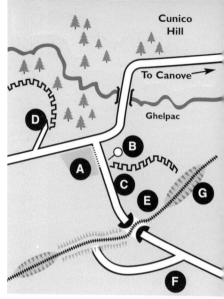

KEY GHELPAC FORK - 4
A. Car Parks and Picnic area
B. Pelly Trench
C. Dug-out/cave
D. Track and Thinle Trench
E. Lay-By and Tunnel
F. Track to railway path
G. Cutting and machine gun post.

was once a shallow basin lined with a number of well preserved trenches, now sadly under many tons of quarry soil. But fortunately there are plenty of undisturbed trenches left in this area. Next to the picnic area is a large notice board listing the forest bye-laws; fairly easy to decipher with an Italian-English dictionary, and worth reading.

Pelly Trench

Face up the track (Princes Road): a trench (**4B**) is on your left, by a track-marker, running up-hill and usually full of forest debris. This was part of Pelly Trench, and originally ran down to the bed of the Gelphac. The trench can be followed eastwards for a considerable (at least two kilometres) distance, to the edge of a new quarry near the village of Roncalto. Fifty metres up the track, on the left, are the remains of a dug-out (**4C**), originally linked to Pelly Trench by a tunnel.

Thinle Trench

A short walk will take the tourist to the remains of Thinle Trench. At the main road, bear left and cross to the other side. About a hundred metres on, is a forest track. This can be followed for about two hundred metres when a well-preserved stretch of trench (**4D**), with dug outs and spurs to weapon-pits. This was part of Thinle Trench, defended by 1/5 Gloucesters during the battle. The trench can be followed for about six hundred metres, until stopped by another new quarry. The task faced

Pelly Cross, 1918. OX & BUCKS LI COLLECTION.

Buco di Cesuna: remains of Thinle Trench.

by the battalion can be clearly seen, as the twists and turns of the trench are not shown on most trench maps. The problems caused by the pitch of the slope are amply demonstrated at nearly every point on the line.

Railway cutting

The track leads to the railway embankment and 'tunnel' (**4E**). Leave the car in the lay-bye on the Ghelpac side of the tunnel. (Beware of large lorries, complete with trailers, both loaded with huge lumps of marble, squeezing through the tunnel.) To avoid a steep scramble, go through the arch and look to the right for a logging track (**4F**) which provides easy access to the railway path. This area was held by the Ox & Bucks during the morning of 15 June 1918, after the forward companies were pushed out of the front line. Follow the railway path into the cutting (**4G**); on the right hand side there is an unusual machine-gun post carved out of rock, with an upper exit to Pelly Trench.

Pelly Cross (5)

Return to the car and continue up Prince's Road for about 200 metres, looking for an open space (**5A**) the junction of some forest tracks - road on the right, and a rough path on the left. This was Pelly Cross, scene of bitter fighting in the afternoon of 15 June. The main track (**5B**) on the right was, in 1918, Pine Avenue, and the path (**5C**) Artillery Road, a spur of Prince's Road, built in May 1918 to allow easy passage of guns to Roncalto Road, and then to positions in No Man's Land to support the intended Allied offensive. (Roncalto Road was originally an extension of Pine Avenue, but only a footpath (**5D**) remains.)

Hill 1021: sunken lane.

Sunken Lane

About 300 metres beyond Pelly Cross a rough road swings to the left. In 1918 (and until 1999) this was a 'sunken lane', but is now a busy marble lorry route; take great care! In June 1918 Battalion Headquarters,

1/4 Ox & Bucks was located here (**5G**).

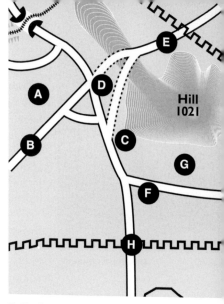

Pelly Cross, Hill 1021, ref (5) on map.

Hill 1021

This is now Hill 1022, and lies above the lane, to the north (left). The slope is fairly gentle, but there are few useful paths, and a lot of undergrowth and some ancient barbed wire, and a some partly-filled in trenches, so take care. Have a look around the area, and reflect on the problems of control during a close-quarter battle in woodland.

Lemerle/Boscon Switch

About 400 metres further along Prince's Road, on the left, can be seen remains of a small quarry. Park, well into the side, and walk back the crest in the road. On either side of the road are remnants of Oxford Trench, part can be followed (with difficulty in places) in either directions for some considerable distance.

Boscon CWGC Cemetery

The cemetery (**6**) lies about 400 metres beyond the quarry site, and again parking can be difficult due to timber lorries. The cemetery contains 146 graves, and the register records the details of 162 burials, including 12 unknown British soldiers, and four Special Memorials. Details are provided in the chapters on memorials and cemeteries, but one interesting grave is that of Lance-Corporal Ernest Brown, 48th Divisional Signal Company, (Wireless Section), killed in action on 15 June 1918. At the time of battle Lance Corporal Brown was in charge of the Wireless Station at the headquarters of 145 Brigade, on the southern slope of M. Lemerle. He stayed at his post during the Austrian artillery bombardment until the wireless station was hit, the set put out of action and he was killed. Also buried here is Lance Corporal Albert

Handley Cross and Rifugio, looking south east.

Fletcher, 48th Divisional Signal Company, RE, a linesman, He spent most of the night of 14/15 June as a member of a working party installing a telephone connection between a machine-gun post in the front line (at the mouth of Happy Valley) and the HQ on M. Lemerle. He was killed about mid-day on 15 June, fighting as an infantryman along with 1/7 Warwicks who were defending the Valle Gap.

Swiss Cottage

Further up (600 metres) the track - somewhere on the right, next to the road - is the site of Swiss Cottage **(7)**, in 1918 an imposing wooden building housing a Field Ambulance. Nothing much can be seen of this amazing building, and as parking is difficult it may not be worth trying to find it without parking at Handley Cross and walking back to rummage in the bush.

Boscon Cemetery.

Handley Cross

The next stop is Handley Cross **(8)**, site of the infamous ammunition dump which exploded on 15th June. In fact there were several dumps in this area, mainly to the south west of the present day *rifugio*. This is a handy spot for lunch: in 1999 a small picnic area was created on the north side of the junction but it is very popular in the summer so stake a claim early, also at the fireplace in the left section of the *rifugio*, although sharing (of a fire) is expected – but not taken for granted – by other visitors. Water, from a rain-catchment system, is available from a *serbatoio* at the back of the shelter. If a thunder storm suddenly appears you will very quickly realize the value of these forest shelters!

Options – All on rough forest tracks

From Handley Cross you can return to Ghelpac Fork, or go eastwards down what was Langabissa Road to Pria dell'Acqua and then to Asiago or Granezza. The forest tracks heading west from Handley Cross are frequently marked as 'closed', and in 2000 were not suitable for a car. If not marked as closed, and you are prepared to risk damage to your car from flying gravel and stones, the right-hand road makes a convenient short cut to the rear slopes of M. Lemerle and the Val Magnaboschi.

CAR AND WALKING TOUR 4:
The Battle in the woods 143 Brigade,
Happy Valley, Valle Gap, Cesuna Ridge, Perghele.

General
Start at Ghelpac Fork car-park **(S)**. Turn left onto the main road and drive towards Cesuna.

Ghelpac Woods
The woods **(1) (2)** on each side of the road saw fierce fighting when the *k.u.k.* pushed the 1/5 Gloucesters back from the front line. As you approach the left hand bend, and if traffic allows, slow down and look to your right, or pull into the rough track **(3)** leading into the quarry workings visible (Q) through the trees. The woods reveal very little of the battle, apart from some remnants of trench above the Ghelpac, but

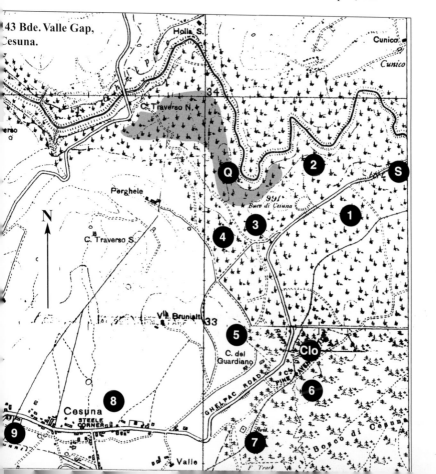

a short walk will allow you to get a feel for the complexities of the front to be defended, and the problems of command and control in woodland warfare, especially direction finding, and detecting the source of hostile small arms fire. During the attack of 15 June 1918, the enemy sited several machine-guns in trees; these were difficult to locate; the British were untrained in forest-fighting whereas the *k.u.k* had practised it for many years. Once located, however, these guns were quickly dealt with by Lewis gun fire, when the guns could be switched from the fleeting but threatening ground targets offered by the assault troops. Also the Austrian uniforms blended with the background, the Official History noted that *the light khaki of the British showing up amid the pines more than the Austrian grey.*

Happy Valley

Happy Valley **(4)** is in front of you, and can be explored but do so with care as there always seem to be logging operations taking place. (The forests are not cleared in this area, only 'pruned', with a few trees extracted at a time.) Again, there is very little to see in the valley, but it is worth a short walk to ponder on the problems of control facing both sides. The attackers seemed to know exactly what to do in this area, possibly confirming that they had conducted good CTR (Close Target Recce) prior to the battle, especially as this area was critical to the success of their offensive in this sector. Return to the car and continue up the road.

Clo [Casello No 7]

The road runs alongside the valley then veers right. After the bend look for, and turn into, the car-park on the left, in front of a large house, (*colonia* - holiday home for children - on modern maps). Casa Guardiano - now 'Guardia' **(5)** is just above the road you have left, on the bank above the road; it is the oldest house among the group on the right. It dominates the shallow hollow, which is the upper end of Happy Valley. Return to the car, and drive across the car-park, heading for the left hand corner.

Clo, or Casello No7 ('15') is a kilometre sign.

The restored building which used to be 'Clo' **(6)** is ahead and to your left, through the trees. To reach the house, drive very

Valle - British artillery position, 15 June 1918, looking west towards Cesuna.

carefully out of the top left hand exit, across a rough stretch of rock-cum-track and onto the railway path. Park under the trees, clear of the path, which is popular with cyclists, horse-riders, motor-cyclists, and walkers. The track to the right of the casello follows the line of Pine Avenue, and can be followed right through the woods to what was Prince's Road.

Valle Gap

Still parked by Clo, turn and face away from the building, and walk up the railway path towards Valle, to get a feel for the terrain. Pause just before an embankment carries a minor road across the railway path. You are now in the vicinity of the Valle Gap **(6)**. The Asiago Tourist Board Great War map shows a military cemetery in this area, this was the *Cimitero Militare Lemerle Capitano Antionio Brandi*, **(7)** containing 1908 graves, but they were exhumed in 1923 and the bones immured in the *Sacrario Militare*. The wire entanglements of the southern end of Cesuna Switch lay here, and just beyond the road lay the spot where the three guns of 12th Battery, XXV Brigade RFA (7th Division), fired over open sights at the advancing enemy, and bombarded C. Guardiano. At this point 1/7 Warwicks under Lieutenant-Colonel Knox met the leading elements of the *k.u.k.* assault and mastered them with small-arms fire in a classic, small-scale encounter battle. From here, or hereabouts, Lieutenant-Colonel Knox directed the field guns to fire on C. Guardiano, then lead some of his men to clear it and turn it into a strong-point to cover the gap with friendly fire. Clo was similarly attacked and occupied. The battalion then attempted to clear the woods towards Perghele, and when that attack was stymied by the enemy, withdrew back to the Gap and joined in the two counter-attacks on the enemy in the forests around Happy

151

Cesuna tunnel.
FRANCIS MACKAY.

Valley and Buco di Cesuna, which speeded their departure.

Cesuna & Steele Corner

Drive back to the main road, turn left and into Cesuna. Take the second major road on the left, at what was Steele Corner **(8)**. Just along on the left is a good delicatessen where the staff speak basic English, and on the right there is a tourist office and small display area where, during the summer, there are occasional interesting exhibitions on the *prima guerra mondiale,* usually around the middle of June. The large car-park at the bottom of this street is on the site of the old railway station; and the tunnel **(9)** where the Battalion Headquarters and a company of 1/5 Warwicks sheltered can easily be found. It is now part of the railway path.

Zovetto Ridge

Drive past the car-park, (down the road from Steele Corner) and follow the black-on-yellow *Cimitero Militare Inglesi,* and the CWGC, signs. Bear right at the next junction, which is really two almost parallel roads and slightly confusing at first sight. Follow the right-hand road up and round through the trees into the Val Magnaboschi. Go past the cluster of houses which comprise the farming hamlet of Magnaboschi, and up to the cross-roads **(10)**. Ignore for the moment the CWGC signs. Turn right and follow the (increasingly twisty) road up to M. Zovetto - watch out for the narrowness of the road, and for the extremely sharp bend off what was Zovetto Avenue onto the track to the Malga Zovetto and *Rifugio* Kubelik **(11)**. Aim to get to the restaurant in the late morning (if you like food); park in the shade of the trees on the south side of the car-park.

The views from the car-park are stunning (see panorama, pages 154, 155). Looking to the right of the *rifugio,* to your front is M. Lemerle, and, slightly right, and higher, M. Magnaboschi. To the right, on the horizon, are M. Ceramella, and M. Pau, the site of a Divisional OP. To the left of M. Lemerle, can be seen Canove, the Val d'Assa (spanned by Roana Bridge), and Roana village. Below the car park to the left of M. Lomerle, the woods around Happy Valley and Perghele can be seen, also Ambrosini (now a cattle breeding station) perched on its hill beyond the start of the Ghelpac Gorge. From the left of the

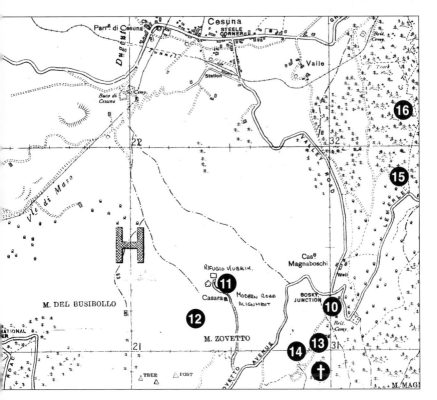

Rifugio, there is a good view of Hill 1140, in 1918 the site of 143 Brigade's OP and Visual Signalling Station, and, in the distance, the rocks and ice of the Gruppo di Brenta, part of the western Dolomites. To the west the woods and a low ridge conceal Unhappy Valley.

Coffee, cold drinks, snacks and ice-cream are obtainable in the restaurant outside of meal times. The main dining room has even better views over the central plain than the car-park. Lunch and dinner, cooked in the sunken grill area, are amazing; but take a hearty appetite as the table d'hôte is not for the sensitive eater, nor for vegans!

M. Zovetto OPs

At one time it was possible to walk to the summit of M Zovetto **(12)**

M. Zovetto: view through embrasure of gallery, M. Magnaboschi.
FRANCIS MACKAY

Rifugio Kubelik, (M. Zovetto): view over the central plain. FRANCIS MACKAY.

M. Zovetto: entrance to defensive gallery built in rocks. FRANCIS MACKAY.

by a path leaving the top-left corner of the car-park. In 1999, this was blocked by the local farmer and remained so in October 2000, but may open again. To get to the site of the British and Italian OPs on the summit drive back down the road and park on the verge just round the first bend after the diary farm, Casara on the map. Walk up the grassy hillside, heading away from the farm. This will bring you to a series of defensive galleries built into rocks on the hillside; they are unusual, and worth exploring. They formed part of the second line of defences built by the Italians, after the *Strafexpedition*. The galleries commanded the Val Magnaboschi, and could be used by machine-gunners, or artillery FOOs, or as really shot-proof communications trenches connecting M. Zovetto, and the supply dumps at Campiello, with the forward positions around Cesuna. Look out for the English

M. Zovetto: Gunners were here (Mbs - 'Master Builders'. RICHARD JEFFS.

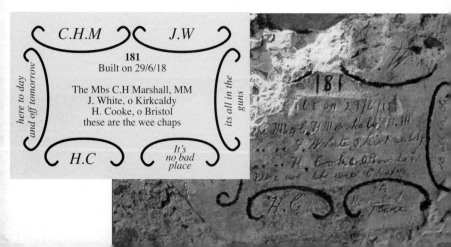

C.H.M   J.W

here to day and off tomorrow

181
Built on 29/6/18

The Mbs C.H Marshall, MM
J. White, o Kirkcaldy
H. Cooke, o Bristol
these are the wee chaps

its all in the guns

H.C   It's no bad place

MOUNT INTEROTTO

ROANA BRIDGE

CANOVE

ROANA

VILLA BRUNIALTI

HAPPY VALLEY

PERGHELE

VALLE GAP

inscriptions traced into the concrete by some artistic British gunners!

The summit of M. Zovetto is a couple of hundred metres above the galleries, and worth the climb. The remains of OPs are easily located; they had an amazing view; artillery observers arriving from France and Flanders must have wondered at their luck (in the summer).

Val Magnaboschi

Return to the valley, park near the chapel at what was Bosry Corner (the adjacent fields are usually used as car-parks during the summer) and walk up the track towards the trees. In the right-hand copse is a *cippo,* an Italian memorial in the shape of a broken Roman column, commemorating the victorious defence of this area by Italian forces during the *Strafexpedition.* Behind the *cippo* is a one time, Italian cemetery, commemorating Italian and Austrian soldiers now a place of commemoration to war dead. **(14)**

It is a beautiful and poignant spot as the name plaques are mounted on white-painted, man-high pine stumps, with Italian and Austrian names appearing on alternate poles. It originally held the remains of 1739 Italian and 596 Austro-Hungarian soldiers.

Opposite is the CWGC Magnaboschi Cemetery, containing more dead from the fighting of 15/16 June 1918 described in the Cemeteries and Memorials section.

Every summer, around 15-17 June, the area between the chapel and the *cippo* is the

Magnaboschi: *Cippo.*
FRANCIS MACKAY

155

Magnaboschi: view of the British cemetery from the Italian-Austrian one.
FRANCIS MACKAY

scene of a pilgrimage organized by the local chapter of the Assocazione Nazionale Fante (National Infantry Association), commemorating the soldiers of all nationalities who died in the vicinity. In recent years the Italian Pilgrims have been joined by representatives from Austria and the UK. There are old soldiers, and young ones, and families, and wine, good food, singing, banners; much laughter and a few tears during the acts of remembrance.

non dimenticateci !

DOMENICA 18 GIUGNO 2000

VII
PELLEGRINAGGIO
INTERREGIONALE DEI FANTI

CESUNA DI ROANA
(altopiano di Asiago-7 Comuni)

M. Zovetto
Val Magnaboschi
M. Lèmerle
ZONA SACRA DEL FANTE

M. Lemerle

Now drive up the forest track opposite the road from M. Zovetto. This will take you close to M. Lemerle; the first turn on the left (once the site of a British Cemetery) after the 'Z' bend was Lemerle Road and it is quite good (for a forest track) but frequently 'disced'. The locals may appear to ignore this, but bear in mind they may work in the forest or have cutting and gathering rights there. Follow this road to where it bends sharp right, park **(15)** and look around on the left for embrasures and some (gridded) *tana di volpe,* and on the right of the road (facing up-hill), the communication trench (C Track) leading south up M. Magnaboschi. A track leads north to the summit of M. Lemerle **(16)**, and more Italian memorials, commemorating the defence of the hill during the *Strafexpedition.*

On the northern slope are the

156

remains of a British OP, entered by a tunnel from the south side of the hill. This tunnel, which doubles as a shelter and rest-area, featured an unusual blast and gas trap at the north end, below the OP; (see sketch). Walk downhill for about one hundred yards, the site can be found - may take a little time.

Return to the car, and head for Cesuna.

Cesuna Switch

Drive back to Steele Corner, **(S)** turn left and follow the road round to the right; the modern road layout is shown in the map. After the lane to the *Cimitero Communale* (on the right), look for a small lay-by/car-park on the left; **(1)** park and cross the road to the fence. This location provides a good view over the site of the Cesuna Switch, and the fighting around Perghele. The switch ran across the ridge to the front, from the Valle Gap, over the meadows to the left of the houses around Casa Guardia, through the strips of woodland on the cemetery side of the Villa Brunialti complex, and down into the combe between Perghele and Casa Traverso South, (prominent corrugated-iron roof). Traverso Trench, the main part of the switch, appears to have disappeared in the

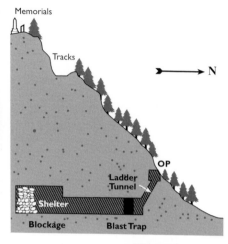

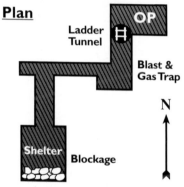

Plan

Cesuna: viewpoints.

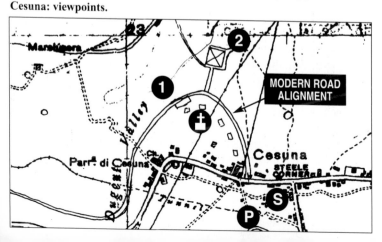

Perghele, view from road near Cesuna cemetery. FRANCIS MACKAY

Twenties, and even on an air-photograph little evidence can be discerned. Even the line of the communication trench running from Thinle Trench, to Perghele and Happy Valley, cannot be located on the ground. For a closer view, walk or drive to the lane leading to the *Cimitero Communale* (2).

Walk around the outside of the cemetery compound, following the lane on the right. In June 1918 the valley between the cemetery and Perghele contained several trench-mortar positions, during the battle the motars bombarded the crossings of the Ghelpac leading to Happy Valley, and concentration areas and forming-up positions used by the *k.u.k.* follow-on forces. Late in the battle a mule-borne section of a 6-inch Newton Mobile Mortar Battery arrived at the hamlet of Cavrari, west of the cemetery. The mule-train travelled from Granezza by way of Longdin Crescent and the Marginal Road, along the edge of the escarpment, to Carriola and then by Cavan Road to Cavrari. The mortars, wooden base blocks, ammunition, tools, etc were taken on by manpower to a point between the two houses mentioned in Car Tour One, at Contra(da) Frighi. A large body of enemy were advancing down Holla Valley towards the Ghelpac crossing. The mortars were hurriedly mounted and ammunition made ready. To the rage of the mortar-gunners, the enemy halted and dispersed into the Austrian equivalent of 'artillery formation', ie spread out over a large area, and sat down - just out of range of the mortars!

The area around the cemetery was used at various times during 15 /16 June 1918 by B Company 48th Bn MGC, but the movements of all detachments was so rapid and dispersed that it is very difficult to relate them accurately to the rest of the battle.

CANOVE

K.U.K. ATTACK ON PERGHELE

K.U.K ATTACK ON HAPPY VALLEY

WOODS ABOVE
HAPPY VALLEY

PERGHELE

1/5 WARWICKS VISUAL
S/G. STATION

Perghele – see map on page 160

The next place to visit is Perghele. In summer the farm operates a riding centre, and light refreshments are usually available, but the (small) car-park can be very busy. It can be reached by car, but the access track is very rough. The easiest way is to walk, starting from the car-park near Clo. **(S)** Walk down the left side of the roads from Ghelpac Fork. After about 150 metres look for a forest track on the left **(1)** and follow it to Perghele. The woods on the left **(2)** were, during, 15 June 1918, full of *k.u.k.* snipers and machine-gun teams, trying to evict the British from Cesuna Switch. The enemy were cleared by the counter-attack of the 1/7 Warwicks lead by Lieutenant-Colonel Knox, later that day.

Look south-west towards Hill 1140, study the land covered by 1/5 Warwicks along Cesuna Switch/Treviso Trench, (and try to imagine the problems of formations reduced to using signal lamps, or semaphore flags, for battle communications between battalions and their brigade headquarters), then turn and look east to see where the *k.u.k.* infantry advanced into the field of fire from RSM Townleys' party. The farm steading at Perghele **(3)** was rebuilt after the war and during demolition of the ruins a large number of British cartridge cases, badges, buttons, and the remains of uniforms, boots and webbing equipment were found under the rubble of that part of the building nearest the access road. This was probably the building where RSM Townley made his stand; by lying down one can appreciate the width of the field of fire obtained from this site. The Italian owners are very broad-minded; if they find you sprawled on the ground peering out at the cow-pasture, just say '*Buon giorno; Ingelsi: grande guerra* *mondiale'*: that will explain everything! Do not pass the house to reach the Col del Vento without permission, usually freely given although, as ever, language can be a problem. If you do pass the farm the view from the (probable) sites **(4)** of the 1/5 Warwicks OP and Visual Signalling Station can be appreciated, also the problem of dead ground to the front of the battalion battle headquarters dug-outs. Do not walk down and into the trees below; the trenches once held by D Company have disappeared into the quarry and entry to any part of the area around dangerous activity is forbidden by a variety of Italian laws.

Casa Guardiano/Guardia

Return towards the main road, but bear right at the first fork and walk past C. Guardiano **(5)** where, despite masking from several new buildings, the dominant position of this house over the Valle Gap, and

Perghele, C. Guardia, V. Brunialti.

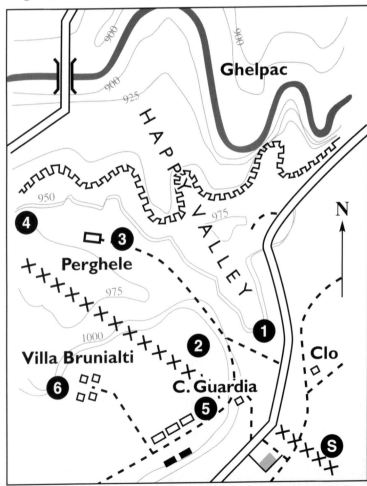

across Cesuna Switch, can be appreciated. Continue along the track.

Villa Brunialti

At the next junction a short detour to the right will let you explore the ground round the Villa Brunialti **(6)**, although there are no clear signs of Treviso Trench. The Villa is a *colonia* (a children's holiday home) and the site of the local high school; if any of the children discover visitors speak English they are experimented on by budding linguists! Return to the main track and then to your car. The track from C. Guardia was, in 2000, private.

Chiesa Museum

There is a small but interesting museum in Tresche-Conca. From Cesuna main (old station) car park, go to Steele Corner, turn left and drive for 2kms to the main Asiago - Strada di Costo road, turn left (carefully; it's a bad junction) and head into Tresche-Conca, going straight on at the roundabout. Turn right at the cross-roads and go up the hill. At the first bend, turn right into the museum, set behind some railings. The collection is displayed on the first floor. It consists of a mock up of an Italian Army hut, and a small display of militaria excavated in the Veneto by the curator, Sr Giancarlo Rovini, who is very helpful but does not speak English. Afterwards, turn right and go up the hill and round the big church and into the small car park next to the *Cimitero Communale*. The views across the Val d' Assa and Val d' Astico are worth a small detour.

Perghele: view from farm steading to 143 Bde HQ OP. FRANCIS MACKAY

Chapter Nine

MEMORIALS & CEMETERIES

Memorials

There are only two war memorials to British forces in the Veneto, one on the plateau, at Granezza, and the other on the banks of the river Piave, in the village of Salettuol. The Piave one commemorates all ranks of the 7th Division who fell in Italy. Many of the Division's casualties in this theatre were incurred in the assault crossing of the Piave 23/27 October 1918. During the Battle of Asiago only the divisional artillery and some infantry working parties, labouring in the rear areas in preparation for the intended Allied offensive, were involved in the battle.

143 (Warwickshire) Brigade Memorial

This memorial is, as mentioned earlier, next to the Granezza cemetery. It is a few yards to the south, set back slightly from the road and in the lea of some rocks. It is dedicated to the memory of

Lt Col Knox.

Lieutenant-Colonel JM Knox DSO, 1/7 Battn Royal Warwickshire Regt, killed in action September 23rd 1918, and Officers, NCOs & men of the 143rd Brigade who fell in action on the Asiago Plateau during 1918. The memorial was commissioned and paid for by the family of Lieutenant-Colonel Knox. He was a native of Nuneaton, and a pre-war member of the 7th Battalion Royal Warwickshire Regiment, TF, which was based in Coventry, with companies in Nuneaton, Rugby and Leamington Spa.

In recent years the memorial has been visited by members of the present-day 143 Brigade, based in Shrewsbury, and by British service personnel from the NATO base in Vicenza, some with connections to the 7th Battalion Royal Warwickshire Regiment TA.

At one stage there were eight battalions of the Royal Warwickshire Regiment in Italy: the 2nd, 1/5th, 1/6th, 1/7th, 1/8th (Territorials), 14th, 15th and 16th (these three all Birmingham Pals).

CWGC Cemetery Registers

There are ninety-three registers for the **Italy 1914-1918** series of cemeteries. Numbers 1-5, 7-11, and 15-93 are useful aids to anyone interested in the British involvement in the fighting north of Venice.

Registers 6, 12, 13 and 14 deal with other areas, such as Taranto, Faenza, Genoa and Arquata which fall outside the scope of this guide. Fortunately Registers 1-5 (Asiago Plateau), and 15-93 (which contain information on many small or single grave locations) are in single volumes. Between 1993 and 1999 poppies were laid by British service personnel as close to Armistice Day as possible to CWGC sites in the Veneto, including most single graves in civil cemeteries.

Giavera Memorial to the Missing

The CWGC cemetery at Giavera, to the east of the town of Montebelluna, houses the memorial to troops recorded as 'missing' in the campaign. The memorial slab is at the western (left, as you enter) end of the cemetery. It bears the words:

TO THE MEMORY OF THOSE OFFICERS, NON-COMMISSIONED OFFICERS AND MEN WHO FELL IN ITALY DURING THE GREAT WAR 1914-1918 AND HAVE NO KNOWN GRAVE.

The memorial was mounted so as to 'command a view' of the Asiago plateau, the Montello, the flood plain of the Piave river, and the Adriatic (just), areas where nearly all of those whose names are recorded on the slab fell. Over the years these 'views' have been obscured by vegetation and some buildings, but in the depths of winter, when the trees are bare, it is possible to catch a glimpse of the escarpment above Bassano del Grappa. The memorial is inscribed with the number, rank, names and probable date when the individual fell. There are 119 names in the memorial register (No 8 in the Italy 1914-1918 series), including those of aircrew lost in the Adriatic after bombing raids on Austrian naval ports in what is now Croatia. Ten of the names are for men lost during the Battle of Asiago, including one Vickers gun team member from 48th Bn MGC, possibly from the team manning the post containing R3 & R4 guns covering the mouth of Happy Valley.

Giavera Cemetery

The cemetery (Register No.7) contains the graves of 417 members of the British armed forces killed in defence of the Montello (winter 1917/18), or died as a result of accidents in the support areas around Montebelluna, during the crossing of the Piave or the pursuit to the Monticano River, 23 October - 4 November 1918.

The cemetery is about seventy kilometres from Asiago, by way of Bassano del Grappa and the S248 to Montebelluna. (Getting around

Bassano can be interesting, but persevere!) Giavera is a large village twelve kilometres to the east of Montebelluna; the cemetery sign-post is on the right-hand side of the road about half way along the main street. The road to the cemetery, the *Via Vittorio*, is on the left. The road twists and turns a bit, and at one point crosses the *Canale Brentele*, an irrigation channel which circumnavigates (almost) the Montello. It was enlarged in 1918-1920 by Austrian prisoners as part of post-war reparations; and is about five metres wide and three deep. The parapet is low so drive carefully near it, especially on a frosty morning.

Keep a sharp look-out for CWGC signs as the last turn is sometimes obscured. Drive up towards, the church, and find a shady spot in the car park on the left. The entrance to the CWGC cemetery is on the opposite side of the road, through a small iron gate. Along a pathway, a joy to the eye in blossom-time, leads to the cemetery, which is very beautiful at any time of the year but especially late summer.

Cemeteries on the Asiago plateau

There are five CWGC cemeteries on the plateau, four in the forests south of Asiago town and one just below the edge of the escarpment. All are easily accessible by car during the late spring, summer and autumn, at least until late November. Thereafter deep snow makes access impossible unless driving a four-wheel drive vehicle. Only the Barental and Magnaboschi cemeteries are accessible throughout the year, but even then only with care in hard weather.

Barental Cemetery

The cemetery contains 125 graves, nine of them unknown British soldiers. The register contains a reference to an 'Unknown Australian Soldier'; maybe a wanderer from the Egypt/Salonika rest camp at Faenza, to the south of Vicenza, near Bologna, who came north seeking adventure or just a mis-spelling of 'Austrian'.

Eighteen of the dead are from the fighting in the woods around San

Barental Cemetery. FRANCIS MACKAY

Sisto Ridge during the Battle of Asiago, or are casualties of the Austrian bombardment; such as three men from the Royal Garrison Artillery: 24033 Serjeant Richard Smyth, MM, MSM, 197th Siege Battery, a native of Plymouth; 111189 Lance-Bombadier Charles William Farmer, of 302nd Siege Battery; and 276960 Gunner Arthur William Price, 307th Siege Battery, aged 35, unmarried, and a native of Preston. The 302nd and 307th Batteries were originally part of the XCIV Heavy Artillery Group, a component of the force of ten newly-raised 6-inch howitzer batteries sent from Aldershot to the Isonzo front in April 1918 in response to a request from the Italians for some artillery support.

Also buried here is 33863 Sapper GA Owen, 23rd Signal Depot, probably killed when the Granezza supply base was hit, or when he was trying to restore air-line contact between Divisional HQ and the forward areas. The Great Cross is sometimes garnished with a wreath of poppies laid by representatives of the Special Forces Club to commemorate the death of the Second World War SOE team leader, Major A J Wilkinson MC RA, killed by German and Italian Fascist anti-partisan forces and commemorated on the Partisan Memorial by the *Osteria di Granezza*.

Boscon Cemetery

Parking here, as on the rest of Prince's Road, is not always easy due to forestry operations. The cemetery contains 162 graves, including twelve men 'Known unto God'. Ninety-six of the entries in the cemetery register are of officers, NCOs and men killed on 15 or 16 June, including three men from 1/South Staffordshire Regiment, part of the 91st Brigade, 7th Division, possibly killed when attached to the 48th Battalion MGC for training but deployed into the line with one or other of the machine-gun teams, or caught by random shellfire in the rear areas, where some men from their battalion were providing working parties as part of the preparations for the intended Allied offensive. The three men, all Private soldiers, are: 39490 William Thomas Alfred Barkby, of Leicester; 235219 Joseph Holmes, of Ulverston; and 41766 CE Pedder.

The other names in the register are for men killed during trench raids in the spring and late summer, or as the result of shelling or accidents. The cemetery occupies the original site of a burial ground serving the left brigade. It was sited within easy reach of the front line, near Queen's Corner, a track junction on Prince's Road, close to 'R', and 'A' Tracks leading from the front line. It was also near the field

Boscon Cemetery. FRANCIS MACKAY

hospital at Swiss Cottage, mentioned in the main text, and to Handley Cross.

One name which jumps out at the reader is that of 341134 Pioneer Fred BV Illingworth, Signal Company, GHQ, RE. He was one of two men from that unit killed on 15 June 1918, possibly attempting to repair the signal circuits destroyed at Handley Cross during the opening barrage and the subsequent explosions and fires. Fred Illingworth was 21 years old when he died. His parents, John Arthur and Ruth Illingworth, were living in Eastbourne at the time, but had emigrated to Britain from Russia some years before the war. They had lived in Pabianice, near Lodz in Russian Poland, where Fred was born, but moved to Moscow before deciding to emigrate. In 1914 Fred was apparently studying at Moscow University but was in England, possibly on vacation, when war was declared and he never saw Russia again. In addition, the two men from 144 Brigade HQ. Wireless Section mentioned earlier, killed when the wireless station on M. Lemerle was hit by artillery fire early in the battle, are buried here.

Also buried in this cemetery is Captain Basil Vassar Bruton, 1/5 Gloucesters, died of wounds on 15 June 1918, possibly the officer in whose pocket was found a leave-pass for Blighty effective from the 16th June.

Five men from 48th Battalion MGC, killed on 15 June 1918 lie here, of the eight reported killed in the battle.

Cavaletto Cemetery

The cemetery lies about five hundred metres off the mountain road which zig-zags down the escarpment from the crossroads at the Rifugio Corno, to Calvene, a pretty little the village in the foothills. In 1918 it was the site of various British supply dumps and support facilities, such as a smithy, vehicle workshops, canteens, baths, and the railhead for a 60 cm gauge light railway line manned by sappers for the 109th Light Railway Operating Company, RE. The line ran from the railway station at Dueville, the British main rail-head, on the standard-gauge branch line from Vicenza to Thiene and Rochette, the start of the rack and pinion line to Campiello.

If contemplating a visit to Cavaletto, read the notes at the end of Car Tour 1 about access and parking.

The cemetery is set in a peaceful hollow on the edge of the escarpment, next to a wood of beech and pine trees. The first burials were in June 1918, and it was completed in 1919 when nineteen bodies were disinterred from M. Sunio cemetery, on the edge of the escarpment, just off the Marginal Road, in a beautiful area overlooking the Venetian plain.

In 1918 the Cavaletto hollow was the site of a some support facilities, including an Advanced Operating Station, where urgent surgical cases - head, lung and abdominal - were treated to avoid the long and arduous journey to the nearest Casualty Clearing Stations, at Montecchio Precalcino and Dueville, villages on the plain, just off the present day A31 Val d' Astico Autostrada. During the battle of 15/16 June a number of casualties succumbed to their wounds in ambulances during or just after that journey, and the AOS was established in late June to prevent any recurrence. (The registers of both cemeteries on the plains contain a number of names from men serving in units engaged in the battle, referred to as 'Killed in action 15 June 1918', or 'Died of wounds 16 June 1918'.) The Prince of Wales visited the AOS shortly after it opened, and noted that it consisted of three huts, and was manned by, among others, five nursing sisters, 'all very plain'!

There are a hundred graves in this quiet and sequestered spot; over sixty of whom are listed as 'Died of wounds'. There are eleven graves for men killed or died of wounds on 15 or 16 June 1918, casualties of the Battle of Asiago and probably all originally buried at M. Sunio cemetery, along with eight others with dates of death around the beginning of July 1918.

One of the casualties of 15/16 June 1918, a member of 8th (Royal Monmouth) Army Troops Company, RE, 266508 Sapper Arthur Chivers Coles, a Yorkshireman from Skipton, not a man of Monmouth. Also buried here, having died of wounds on 15 June 1918, is 197916 Sapper Tommy Charles Baines, 'J' Company, HQ Signal Company, RE, and native of Antwerp, Belgium, with an English father and Belgian mother. Tommy had enlisted in the British Army on 1 November 1914.

Cavaletto cemetery receives fewer visitors than the others on the plateau, but is worth the small amount of trouble required to locate parking and turning points.

Granezza Cemetery

The cemetery houses the remains of 142 men, including three 'Known Unto God'. It was completed after the Great War, when thirty-four bodies were removed to it from three outlying British cemeteries, one on M. Kaberlaba, another near M. Langabissa and the third at the side of Barental Road, north of Pria dell'Acqua crossroads and below M. Sprunch. Granezza cemetery contains numerous graves from the fighting of 15/16 June and Edward Brittain lies in Grave 1, Plot 1, Row B. There are often flowers at the foot of his gravestone or on the Grand Cross.

Magnaboschi Cemetery

This is a very fine cemetery, set in the deep, still, Val Magnaboschi. Normally the only sounds to be heard are the wind rustling the woods, the occasional baa-ing of sheep, or cow-bells from the herds belonging to the *Casara Zovetto*. The beasts roam the valley, and the slopes above, between mid-May and September, when they are driven into sheltered ground and byres for over-wintering. The area around the British and the Italian cemeteries is very quiet - except during the week-end closest to 15 June! The cemetery was opened in 1923, and contains the remains of soldiers disinterred from two smaller sites, one by Valle, the other at a bend in the track (Lemerle Road) which ran from Bosky Corner to M. Lemerle; both cemeteries are shown on the map on page 153. The cemetery contains the remains of 183 war dead, and the register holds the names of 180, and notes the presence of three 'Known Unto God'. Many (124, possibly 125, as one body remains unidentified, the date of death recorded as 'believed to be 15th June 1918') were casualties from the fighting of 15/16 June 1918, killed in the fighting along the Cesuna Switch, in the Valle Gap or by artillery in the woods behind Happy Valley. Second-Lieutenant Thomas Lorde Goode, of Hinckley, the Intelligence Officer of 1/5 Royal Warwicks, is buried here (Grave 1.C.11), as is Major Bindloss (Grave 1.C.13), and eleven of their comrades-in-arms from 1/5 Royal Warwicks, mainly killed in the fighting around Perghele and in the trenches overlooking Happy Valley.

The cemetery is the last resting place for ten members of 1/7 Royal Warwicks, killed around the Valle Gap, but only one member of 48th Bn MGC, (and one from the 7th Battalion, possibly attached to the 48th for training) probably from the gun teams covering the point where the Austrians stormed over the Ghelpac and across the wire at the mouth of Happy Valley. Various accounts of the battle indicate that

Magnaboschi Italian and British Cemeteries c. 1922; note Cippo, left.
VITTORIO CORA COLLECTION.

the machine-gun post (two teams, R4 and R5 guns) was destroyed, and all men killed, wounded or missing. The sergeant in charge was found dead in the act of reloading his revolver, this must have been 18373 Lance-Sergeant James Leyden Cochrane, from Hawick, in the Scottish border country, the only senior MGC NCO buried on the plateau (in Boscon cemetery), and with a date of death for the day of the battle. The 48th Battalion MGC Battle Narrative counts 8 dead, and 15 missing in action plus 43 wounded, but does not list names.

One feature of the inscriptions is the relatively advanced age of some of the private soldiers killed in the battle, for example: 37356 Corporal Henry Charles Baker, aged 35 years; 241855 Private Henry Sidney Bond, 1/5 Gloucestershire Regiment, aged 34 years. 39266 Private James Grimston, 1/6 Gloucestershire Regiment, aged 35 years; 27/293 Private William Gatiss, 11/Northumberland Fusiliers, aged 40 years; 29350 Private John William Hines, 1/8 Royal Warwicks, aged 39 years; and others, yielding a total for this cemetery alone of twenty-seven men over 30, out of 139 identified bodies of infantrymen holding a rank below sergeant. The job of an infantryman is always arduous, even in the 21st Century, and in 1918 it was very demanding, physically and mentally. The older men may have had the mental resilience to cope with many aspects of front-line service but they would have found prolonged, arduous labour at altitudes over 3,000 ft above sea level very demanding.

Towards the rear of the cemetery, on the right-hand side, in Plot 3,

Row G Grave 1, lies 291011 Private Andrew Dutch, 2/Gordon Highlanders. This grave caught the writer's eye during his first visit to the plateau. At the bottom of the gravestone is inscribed 'SON OF W. DUTCH, LUTHER MAINS, KINCARDINESHIRE, SCOTLAND'. This farm lies close to the small town of Laurencekirk, close to the A90 Dundee - Aberdeen road. The Mains of Luther ('Luuther', rather than Loo-ther) farm is set a few hundred yards off the A90, and close to the small community of Luthermuir, set in the rich farmland of the Mearns, an area described vividly in *The Scots Quair* (Quire), a trilogy of farming life written in the Twenties by Lewis Grassic Gibbon, and published in 1932. The book describes life in the Mearns, before and during the Great War. Andrew Dutch was one of several children living at the Mains of Luther and his boyhood is probably mirrored in *The Scots Quair*. He had many friends among the children living in the surrounding farms and in the cottages of Luthermuir. Andrew 'went for a sojer' in 1915 and joined the Gordon Highlanders. He went with 2/Gordons on the long journey to Italy, and eventually to the Asiago Plateau, where he served with D Company. On 15 July 1918, the battalion took over the Cesuna section of the front line. D Company was right support company, in the vicinity of the Valle Gap and Clo. The following day the company was hit by an enemy artillery strafe, and suffered three dead, one of them Andrew Dutch. In the late 1990s his nephew, William Dutch, living until recently not far from the Mains of Luther, could recall his parents talking about the young man who went off to the wars and failed to return; killed 'in something to do with a railway'.

At one time the writer regularly passed the Luther road-end while taking a short-cut to Deeside. The sight of a familiar and homely name on a gravestone from a forgotten campaign was startling, and initiated a train of events which lead to this guide. However, there is another twist to this small coincidence. Andrew had a boyhood friend in Luthermuir, Tom Gibb. Tom joined the RFC, and was posted to Italy with 34 Squadron. The squadron moved around a bit, but spent some time at Villaverla airfield, a few miles from Dueville. 99434 Air Man

Dueville CWGC Cemetery. FRANCIS MACKAY

(sic) 2nd Class Thomas Ritchie Gibb, son of Edmund Gibb, of Luthermuir, died on 30 November 1918, of pneumonia and lies in the CWGC Cemetery in Dueville, a small town on the Venetian plain between the escarpment and Vicenza. Tom's grave is almost within sight of Andrew's, as the escarpment is visible from Dueville. Both boys are commemorated on the Parish of Aberluthnot war memorial: as are another Private Dutch and a second Private Gibb.

War memorial, Parish of Aberluthnot, Kincardineshire.
FRANCIS MACKAY

The writer came across Tom Gibb's grave while making arrangements for an Armistice ceremony at Dueville cemetery, the nearest to the NATO base at Vicenza. Unfortunately a piper was unobtainable for that ceremony, but, as at Magnaboschi, the sight of a familiar name in a place far from the Howe o' the Mearns, and memories of flocks of sheep and cowbells in the Val Magnaboschi, brought to mind the words of that most haunting of laments for the fallen, *The Flo'ers o' the Forest:*

> *I've heard the lilting at our ewe-milking,*
> *Lassies are lilting before dawn of day;*
> *But now they are moaning, on ilka greenloaning;*
> *For the flo'ers o' the forest are a' wede away .*

Further reading

Barnett, G.H., *With the 48th Division in Italy;* Edinburgh & London, 1923

Bairnsfather, B., *From Mud to Mufti*

Caddick-Adams, P., *By God they can fight!: History of 143 Brigade;* Shrewsbury, 1997

Carrington, C.F., *The War Record of the 1/5 R. Warwickshire Regt*

Cassar, George H., *The Forgotten Front, the British Army in Italy, 1917-1918;* London, 1998

Crutwell, C., *The War Service of the 1/4 Royal Berkshire Regt (TF);* Oxford, 1922 (BL)

Dalton, E. H. J. H., *With British Guns in Italy;* London, 1919

Dopson, F.W., *The 48th Signals in the Great War;* Bristol, 1938

Eberle, V. F., *My Sapper Venture;* London 1973

Edmonds, J. E., *Official History of the War Military Operations Italy 1915-1919;* London, 1986

Gladden, Norman, *Across the Piave;* London, 1971

Greenwell, Graham, *An Infant in Arms;* 1935

Herwig, H.H., *The First World War; Germany and Austria-Hungary*

1914-1918; London, 1997

Mockler-Ferryman, A.F., *The Oxfordshire and Buckingham LI Chronicle*

Pickford, P., *War Record of the 1/4 Ox & Bucks LI;* Banbury, 1919

Sandilands, H. R., *The 23rd Division 1914-1918;* Edinburgh, 1925

Stacke, H.F.M., *The Worcestershire Regiment in the Great War*

Ward, S.G.P., *Faithful: The Story of the Durham Light Infantry;* London, 1962

Wilks, J. and Wilks, E. M., *The British Army in Italy 1917-1919;*
              Barnsley, 1998

Wright, P.L., *The First Buckingham Battalion 1914-19*

Wyrall, R.E., *The Gloucestershire Regiment in the War 1914-18;* Methuen
              1931

Reference Material

Public Record Office, *Kew,* London

File References, *War Diaries, 1914-1922,* Part II Italy

Campaign in general, *WO95: 4194 - 4260*

Selection for Asiago
23rd Division, HQ/HQ Troops   4229-4234
68 Inf BDE HQ. 4235
70 Inf BDE HQ.
11/ Sherwood Foresters 4240
8/ KOYLI 4240
8/ Y&L 4240
9/ Y&L 4240
48th Division HQ/HQ Troops
143 Inf BDE (all units/formations) 4244-4247
144 Inf BDE (all units/formations) 4249
145 Inf BDE (HQ 4250)
1/1 Bucks. 4251
1/4 Oxf & Bucks. 4251
4/ R. Berks. 4251
1/5 Gloucs. 4251

Maps from the campaign: WO 369 series
WO 369/201 Asiago sheet FO 37 IV SO
WO 369/202 Asiago shet FO 37 IV SW
1:25,000
WO 369/334 Asiago: BR and AM Trenches April 1918

INDEX